THE HORSE INTERLUDE

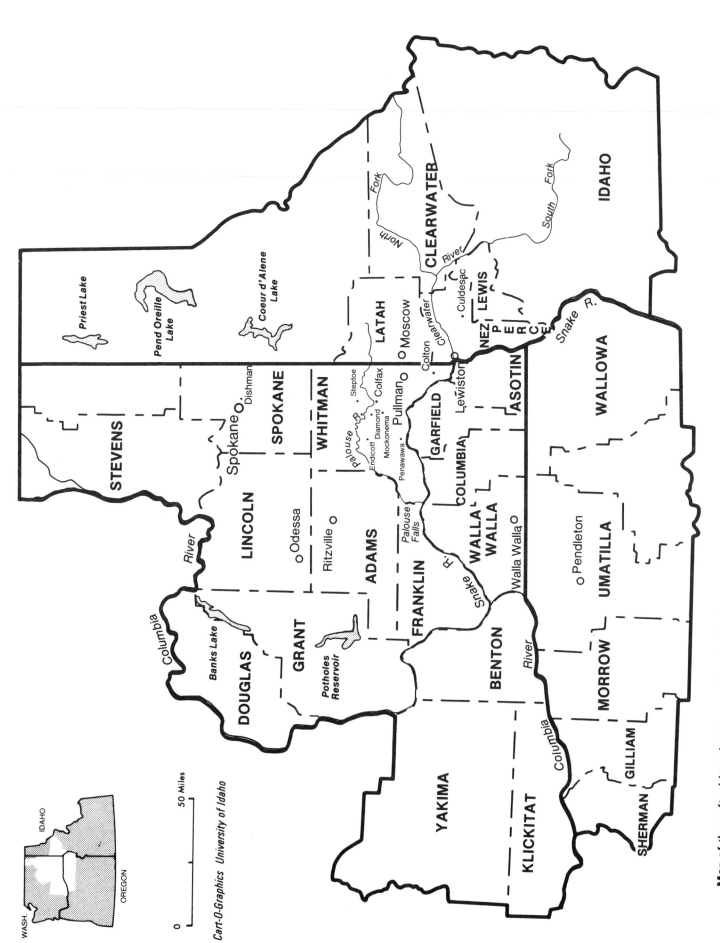

Map of the soft white wheat area of the Pacific Northwest. Prepared by Alan A. DeLucia, Director of Cart-O-Graphics, University of Idaho.

Cart-O-Graphics University of Idaho

50 Miles

IDAHO

WASH.

OREGON

STEVENS

LINCOLN

DOUGLAS

GRANT

ADAMS

FRANKLIN

SPOKANE

WHITMAN

LATAH

CLEARWATER

IDAHO

LEWIS

NEZ PERCE

ASOTIN

GARFIELD

COLUMBIA

WALLA WALLA

BENTON

YAKIMA

KLICKITAT

SHERMAN

GILLIAM

MORROW

UMATILLA

WALLOWA

Priest Lake

Pend Oreille Lake

Coeur d'Alene Lake

Banks Lake

Potholes Reservoir

Spokane

Dishman

Odessa

Ritzville

Steptoe

Diamond

Endicott

Mockonema

Colfax

Penawawa

Pullman

Moscow

Colton

Culdesac

Clearwater

Lewiston

Walla Walla

Pendleton

North Fork

South Fork

River

Clearwater River

Snake R.

Snake River

Palouse R.

Palouse Falls

Columbia River

Columbia River

Columbia River

THE HORSE INTERLUDE

A Pictorial History of Horse and Man
in the Inland Northwest

by
Thomas B. Keith

Edited by
Clifton Anderson

Illustrated by Greg Pole

THE UNIVERSITY OF IDAHO PRESS

The University of Idaho Press
Moscow, Idaho

Cover and interior illustrations by Greg Pole

Library of Congress Catalog No. 76-46792
ISBN 0-89301-036-7

DEDICATED TO MY
MOTHER, LOTTIE MAY HAYS KEITH
AND
FATHER, ANDREW NOLAN KEITH

PREFACE

My parents moved from Pike County, Missouri, to Endicott, Washington, in 1902. In 1905, my father rented 320 acres eight miles southwest of Colfax, Washington, near Mockonema in township 16, section 22 (see map, page 14). It was here that my first lessons in horsemanship began when I was eight years old. Horses were hitched to plows, grain drills, harrows, headers, combines, wheat wagons, and other farm machines.

In 1910, at the age of 13, I drove a header wagon for a period of 25 days. During this harvest period, fires destroyed the great white pine forest of the Northern Idaho area. The days were extremely hot with smoke hovering low above us. The horses suffered considerably from the heat and smoke. This situation taught me many lessons of horsemanship and horse psychology.

I learned to drive plow teams of six, seven, eight, and nine horses. At the age of 18 I was given the opportunity to be a header driver or "puncher".

In 1918, my father purchased a McCormick header, a Case separator, and a non-tractible International engine. (This engine had to be moved with horses.) In 1919, he purchased a Rumely Oil-Pull gas engine. We operated this outfit from 1918 to 1925. I punched the header when it was possible to hire a machinist to operate the engine and separator. If we could not hire a machinist, I would tend the engine and separator and hire a man to punch the header. During one harvest season, I drove a push binder.

I was graduated from the University of Idaho in 1924 with a degree in animal husbandry, received a master's degree in 1926 from the University of Illinois, and a Doctor of Philosophy in nutrition in 1933 from Pennsylvania State University. I taught courses in animal science at Pennsylvania State University from 1927 to 1942. From 1942 to 1946, I served in the U.S. Army as a food, nutrition, and agricultural specialist in U.S. and the European Theatre of Operation. My assignment in France and Germany was concerned with food and general agriculture problems. I taught animal science courses in Montana State University for a period of 16 months. From July, 1947, to retirement in 1966, I was a member of the Department of Animal Science at the University of Idaho. There, I taught courses in nutrition and conducted nutritional research with cattle, sheep, and swine.

Through the years, I have had many occasions to tell various audiences about agricultural developments in the Northwest. While I was at Pennsylvania State University, my colleagues and associates often asked me for information about the large teams used in Northwest wheat fields. Partly to satisfy their curiosity, I began collecting photos of the big teams in action. Year by year, my collection of photos has grown. During my teaching career, I enjoyed sharing my information and photos with students. Now, for those readers who wish to examine a bygone era of agricultural history, I am pleased to once more assume the role of interpreter of "The Horse Interlude."

Thomas B. Keith

University of Idaho
Moscow, Idaho
October 1, 1976

5

Acknowledgements

I am deeply indebted to many individuals who supplied me with information not available in libraries and who were especially interested in this historical presentation of a rare situation involving a contribution of man in an environment ideal for wheat and horses.

First, I must acknowledge a debt to my father who taught me the basic principles of horsemanship required to produce wheat.

Special mention of contribution is due to:

J.W. Martin, emeritus, Head of the Department of Agricultural Engineering, University of Idaho, for encouragement, suggestions, and valuable pictures.

George W. Woodbury, J. T. Dvorak, Roscoe D. Watson, and Clifford W. Ott for their help with photographs.

Gainford W. Mix for pictures and information pertaining to the origin and development of the Idaho National Harvester.

Ann Wallace for the suggestion of the title and recommendations relative to organization of the subject.

Mary Ruth Koehler for editorial suggestions.

Richard C. Walter for the many pictures of combines and other farm teams.

W.C. Loney for pictures and information pertaining to the operation of combines.

R. Bruce Bray, Secretary of the University of Idaho Faculty, and his staff, Kathleen Probasco, Marlyn Munns, Leslee Holt, and Toni Koubourlis, for the typing of the manuscript.

George B. Hatley for photos and information relative to the Appaloosa horse.

Alan A. DeLucia, Director, Cart-O-Graphics, University of Idaho College of Mines, for preparing the geographic orientation maps.

Lester Kimberling for photos and information on horses and sketches for harness.

Carl J. Kiilsgaard for photos and information on horses.

Gregory Pole, artist, for cover paintings and the redrafting of harness drawings.

TABLE OF CONTENTS

INTRODUCTION

The "Horse Interlude" presents a pictorial history of the horse in the soft white wheat area of the Pacific Northwest. The interlude began when the horse replaced the cradle and flail with the reaper and ended when the self-propelled combine replaced the horse. This includes the period from approximately mid-1850s to the 1930s.

The term "soft white wheat area" originated from the fact that the variety of wheat specifically adapted to the environment of the area produced a soft, white kernel low in the percentage of protein and high in the percentage of starch.

In addition to being an ideal environment for the production of white wheat, the temperature, precipitation, and type of vegetation contributed to an ideal environment for the life cycle of the horse.

The soil was especially adapted to wheat production. According to the soil authorities of the area, the soil of the soft white wheat area was one of the richest in plant food of the world at the time man arrived in the area. It was estimated that there was sufficient plant food in the soft white wheat area to produce wheat for 60 years without fertilization.

THE AREA

The geographical setting of my story is the soft white wheat area of the Northwest. Although hard red wheat is grown extensively in the wheat country east of the Rocky Mountains, a different type of wheat flourishes in a fertile area of the Northwest. Here, environmental conditions are suitable for the type of wheat mentioned above. Some varieties of soft, white wheat are planted in the fall, where moisture supply is adequate and winter conditions are not too severe. Other varieties are seeded in the spring.

The soft white wheat area includes a geographical section located along the Snake River in Idaho, Washington, and Oregon. This area is west of the Rocky Mountains and east of the Cascade Mountains. It includes Whitman, Lincoln, Adams, Grant, Walla Walla, Douglas, Spokane, Columbia, Benton, Garfield, Franklin, Klickitat, Yakima, and Asotin counties of the State of Washington; Latah, Nez Perce, Idaho, Clearwater and Lewis counties of the state of

Idaho; and Umatilla, Morrow, Gilliam, Sherman, and Wallowa counties of the state of Oregon.

In addition to being an ideal environment for the growing of soft white wheat, the temperature, precipitation, and type of vegetation contributed to an ideal environment for the life cycle of the horse. The areas bordering the Snake and Columbia rivers are warm during the winter months (January and February), are well protected from storms, and have an early growth of vegetation in the spring season followed by a late summer growth in the high altitude areas. The vegetation matures into an ideal feed for the horse during the autumn and early winter seasons.

The indigenous vegetation was predominately blue bunch wheatgrass (Agropyron inerme). Blue bunch wheatgrass contained sufficient quantities of all the nutrients required of the horse for all seasons and all stages of the development of the horse.

HOW THE HORSE WAS USED

In the history of the area, the horse's role in wheat farming was distinctly different during three time periods. In each case, the division between one period and the next was marked by technological innovations which enabled farmers to carry out farming operations with increased efficiency. Technology was progressing rapidly. New machinery was introduced — and farmers of the area employed much ingenuity in adapting the new machines for their particular needs.

Ways of using the horse changed during these three periods of agricultural history in the Northwest:

1. **Settlement by Pioneers.** To harvest and thresh wheat, the first settlers used traditional hand implements — the cradle and the flail. Harvesting became semi-mechanized when the horse-drawn McCormick reaper was introduced. In pioneer-day threshing, the horse was sometimes used for trampling the cut grain on a hay mow floor. This was a primitive method for loosening the kernels from the spike of the wheat plant. I review the early days of wheat farming in Part I of this book. Before farmers settled the land, the horse had served the transportation

needs of the people in this area. The famous Indian horse, the Appaloosa, had an influence on agricultural development. So did the horses which pulled wagon trains to Army posts and early mining camps. I trace these influences in Part I.

2. **The Beginning of Large-Scale Farming.** Although inventors throughout the U.S. were experimenting with labor-saving farm implements in the 19th century, many of the inventions found widespread acceptance only in the West. The gang plow is an example. It became popular in the Pacific Northwest, while farmers in the other parts of the country found it to be unsuitable for their soil conditions and farming operations. Northwest farmers used multiple-hitch teams to pull plows, harrows, and drills. They became skilled in hitching and handling teams of six, eight, 10, or more horses. This was the beginning of large-scale wheat farming. I discuss this development in Part II.

3. **The Triumph of Mechanization.** The wheat farmers' ability to use big teams made possible some major breakthroughs in mechanized harvesting. In Part III, I describe the origin and development of the combine-harvester along with the use of the multiple hitch (Schandoney equalizing hitch) for teams pulling these combines.

The story of threshing is my topic in Part IV. I describe the origin, development, and operation of the stationary thresher. This threshing rig included a source of power, either an engine or horses, and a separator which separated the kernels from the straw and chaff. The first separators were powered by horses attached to a sweep. Later, steam and internal combustion engines came into use.

The header, a harvesting machine pushed by horses, was used extensively in the steeply sloping wheat fields of the Northwest. I present the history of the header in Part V, together with comparative information about pull binders and push binders. Using headers, harvesting crews could cut fully ripe wheat and save more of the grain than would have been the case if binders had been used. This was important in localities where environmental conditions favored the growth of varieties of wheat that ripened during a short period of time. The ripe wheat would shatter badly, if not handled gently. The header cut the wheat plant with 10 to 12 inches of straw and elevated it to a wagon box of unusual design. This was the "header box" — and here the wheat was piled carefully, for transport to a threshing site.

There was one horse-propelled harvesting machine which was especially suited to the conditions of the soft white wheat area because it combined the labor-saving features of the big combines with the maneuverability of the push-type binder and header. This was the Idaho National Harvester, a combine harvester designed and built in Moscow, Idaho. I tell the story of this remarkable machine in Part VI. Light in weight and easily maneuverable, this machine could be operated by two men and eight horses. Successful combines of this type eliminated the need for service threshermen.

Horses had names, of course, and in Part VII the names and histories of some outstanding horses of the area are called to mind. I also recall the accomplishments of the Northwest's great horsemen and horsewomen. Reared within the area during the era in which the horse was the main source of power, these people had unusual abilities. They were capable of training the horse for a greater variety of performances than was the case for riders and trainers in any other section of the world.

In the present, horses and horsemanship continue to be important elements in the Northwest's way of life. Our agriculture has moved into the post-horse era — and I review some of the changes in Part VIII. Fortunately, horse and man are partners in many recreational activities today. I conclude my history with a view of the horse as a resource for recreation.

Part One
PIONEER DAYS

The early waves of westward emigration passed by the soft white wheat area. Attractive land for farming was available elsewhere — and the discovery of gold in California lured many emigrants in that direction. By 1856, a few venturesome pioneers had become established in the area. Many more were to follow. E.D. Pierce's rich gold strike at Orofino Creek in 1860 attracted to Idaho gold-seekers from West and East. The gold rush in British Columbia was another incentive for miners and other emigrants to penetrate the area.

Farmers who pioneered in the settlement of northeastern Oregon, eastern Washington, and western Idaho could sell horses and mules to miners who were passing through or were working claims in the region. Getting crops to market was a major problem. Transportation was difficult in the early days and distant markets did not become accessible until construction of the western railroads was completed.

Walla Walla, Washington, was an important center of early settlement. Here, grain growing has a long history. In 1861, there were 4,000 to 5,000 acres of wheat and oats harvested within a 15-mile radius of Walla Walla. This was about all the grain grown at that time in the Inland Empire (that portion of the Pacific Northwest east of the Cascade Mountains). In the Palouse region of eastern Washington and western Idaho, grain growing became fairly important in the 1870's.

My parents' farm was in the Palouse, near Colfax, Washington. Settlement of this area came about in the Post-Civil War years, as indicated by the early place-names. Rebel Flat, named for a Southerner who settled there, was paralleled six miles farther west by a settlement area which was called Union Flat in honor of a Northerner. In 1870, there were 118 people living north of the Snake River on Union Flat; 10 years later, the population had risen to 7,014. Whitman County was designated a county in 1871.

Located near river navigation, the Palouse had some early-day advantages in regard to transportation. In 1875, grain from Colfax was hauled down the long Almota hill to river boats. This must have been a difficult trip for the teamsters and also for the horses and mules which pulled the freight wagons. An exciting innovation was made in 1877, when a chute was constructed from the top of the hill all the way down to the Snake River. Sacks of wheat moved down this chute and were loaded on the river boats. This is an example of the resourcefulness and ingenuity of the early wheat farmers.

The first train did not reach Colfax until November 10, 1883. This was 14 years after the first transcontinental railway was completed, with the last spike uniting the Union Pacific and the Central Pacific being driven near Ogden, Utah, on May 10, 1869. From Colfax, the railroad line was extended to Moscow, Idaho — a distance of 26 miles. Two years were required for this project.

By 1883, the Northern Pacific had extended its main line across northern Idaho and Washington, linking the Great Lakes and the West Coast. Northern routes were followed by other transcontinental lines constructed in this period. These railroads served the new city of Spokane, incorporated in 1878. Spokane experienced rapid growth and became the major trade and transportation hub of the Inland Empire. In 1870, the entire population of what is now Spokane County was only 29. Ten years later, the county's population had grown to 4,262. The 1900 census showed 36,843 persons living in the city of Spokane.

It was during the 1890s that emigration to the Pacific Northwest gained great momentum. Many settlers of this decade established wheat farms. During three previous decades, the early pattern of wheat farming had been shaped by pioneer settlers.

HORSES FOR FARMING, FREIGHTING, AND CONSTRUCTION

Before they became involved in breeding horses for wheat farming, settlers of the Northwest were supplying horses and mules for freighting and road construction.

The Palouse area — which eventually became the center of the soft white wheat area — had a flurry of activity after 1860, with prospectors and miners going to or returning from the placer gold

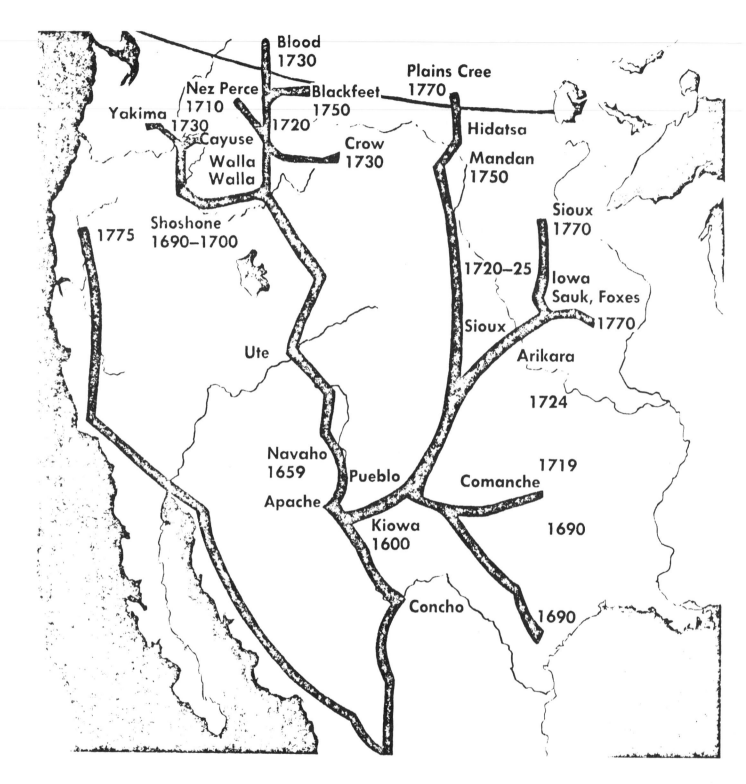

Fig. 1. Northward Spread of the Horse in the United States

mines in western Montana and British Columbia. The miners were followed by thousands of settlers moving into the area in search of farming lands and stock ranches.

Road construction and freight wagons increased the need for horses. The topography of the area required considerable work and time for road construction.

The Mullan Road[2] was one of the first and most important of the roads. It was surveyed and built between 1859 and 1862. Work on the stretch of 624 miles required the use of 10,000 pack mules, in addition to those used during the survey and grading.

The Mullan Road connected Fort Benton, Montana, the head of navigation on the Missouri River, with Walla Walla, Washington, near the navigable waters of the Columbia River.

As a transportation artery, the Mullan Road was primitive and often difficult to travel over, but it did open the area for settlement. It also stimulated within the area the development of a horse-production industry.

Wagon trains were the principal form of overland transportation before the coming of the railroads. When long distances were covered by a wagon train, teams of oxen were generally used. The cattle could live on native vegetation, while horses and mules would require supplementary feed. Many Idaho freighting companies used "10-by-10" outfits; these consisted of 10 wagons with 10 span of oxen for each. On longer runs, they would use the "bull outfit" which had 25 freight wagons and a mess wagon.

The oxen's superior adaptability to trail conditions is the reason they were preferred to horses for pulling covered wagons over the Oregon Trail. The ox has a stomach system which is adapted to the utilization of the natural vegetation without the need for concentrates such as oats, barley, and corn. The ruminant has a large stomach with four divisions, which contains billions of micro-organisms capable of converting coarse fibrous material to usable energy. The horse does not have this system and requires feeds of low fiber content.

For this reason, a limited number of horses survived the trip to their destination over the Oregon Trail, even though they were not required to pull a load. The percentage of survival would depend upon the available moisture for forage growth. An ideal fresh forage cover would

be favorable to horse survival. One owner of a group of wagons began his trip with 12 Percheron mares and a stallion. He reached his destination with only three mares.[3]

The horses that did survive the trip west found a favorable environment in the soft white wheat area. Due to the climate and the type of native vegetation, the area was well suited to the raising of horses. Throughout the Pacific Northwest, farmers found it profitable to keep brood mares. Some large-scale breeding farms were set up. The Oregon Horse and Land Company, headquartered in Baker County, had the reputation of being the largest horse raising company in North America.[4] This company branded 8,000 horses in 1884 and almost 11,000 in 1885. According to one author, "It was not uncommon for a rancher or a breeder to ride a hundred miles to buy a horse from a member of this company; horse thieves would ride clear across the state to steal one!"

Horses came west not only with the settlers' wagon trains but also aboard ships that sailed around Cape Horn. In the latter part of the century, there were even shipments from Europe. The Oregon Horse and Land Company, for instance, imported more than 100 Percherons from France.

In the early part of the 19th century, European horses were brought to the Northwest by representatives of the Hudson's Bay Company. Some descendants of these horses undoubtedly contributed to the agricultural development of the region.

As early as 1845, the Willamette Valley was reported to have 1,716 horses of Clydesdale, Percheron, and Belgian breeding.[10] For the entire Oregon Territory, the census report for 1869 listed these numbers of animals:

48,800	horses
1,560	mules and asses
79,312	milk cows
101,960	sheep
117,700	swine
140,500	young cattle

Long before the white man's arrival in the Pacific Northwest, Indians of the region had made horsemanship an important part of their way of life. Their horses were of Spanish and Austrian stock. The horses were the legacy of early Spanish explorers, first introduced into the Southwest and later brought into areas which the

PLAT OF
TOWNSHIP 16 NORTH, RANGE 42 EAST, W.M.
WHITMAN COUNTY, WASH.
Scale 2 Inches = 1 Mile

References:
Railroad
Wagon Road
Creek
Trail
Numbers with circles 7 indicate the adjoining page or the number of page on which a larger scale map will be found.

37

F.D. Garrett
F.V. Waldrip Lessee
F.D. Garrett Lessee
S. Quigley Hrs Fred Quigley Lessee 440.01
W.P. Slipe
C.W. Hamilton
E.B. Paul Lessee
Wm Guske
Burrell Inv. Co.
W.L. Ripley 163.54
Diamond
O.R. & N. R.R.
H.T. Lamb

6
5
J.W. Hodgen 160
4
C.N. Stilson 480
3
M.B. Larrick 195
2
William Huntley 360
1

F.W. Ertel 280
E.E. Ertel Lessee
Frank N. Day 160
C.N. Stilson 195.99
C.N. Stilson 160

C.F. Jinderlee 285

B.F. Smith 240
J.W. Day 160
J.E. Creuzer 120
C.N. Stilson 320 W.W. Stilson Lessee
W.P. Slipe 40
Geo. Horton 280 L.F. Hubbard Lessee
J.F. Armfield J.F. Creuzer Lessee
John Erford 320
Phillip Andrea 160
C.B. Morley 320

7
8
9
10
11
12

J.S. Mullens 80
H.S. Harris 160
C.L. Chamberlain Wm Sellers Lessee 160
F.A. Davis 40 T.J. Besold Lessee
Wm Huntley 320
H.F. Schreiber 320
L.F. & A.W. Kasdorf 160

G.H. Thomas 80
40
120
Geo. Horton 160
Fred A. Schreiber 320
Fred A. Schreiber
H.F. Schreiber
Marion Freeman to O.S. Jones (Con.) 180
D.L. Taylor 160

18
Wm Huntley 280 Wm Besold Lessee
17 Wm Huntley 520
16 Wm Huntley 640
15
14 360
13

N.M. Whealen 80
Wm Huntley 160
Frank H. Schreiber 120
Marion Freeman 140
John O'Neil 160

29

G. Hubbard Est. Lessee
J.F. Whealen 320
J.F. Whealen
Wm Huntley 160
Wm Huntley 320
A.C. Smith 320 A.N. Keith Lessee
Frank H. Schreiber 199
Burrell Inv. Co. 120
Marion Freeman 200

31

19
J.F. Whealen 40
20
R.T. Whealen
21
22
23
24

N.M. Whealen 160
Jas. A. Whaelan 160
Wm McNeilly 160
E. Krueger 320
Frank E.H. Schreiber 80
F.G. Diercks 160
Geo. Luther 160
E.H. Duckett 160

G. Hubbard Est. Tom Hubbard Lessee
J.F. Whealen
N.M. Whealen 40 J.A. Whealen 40
J.F. Whealen 80
Wm McNeilly 80
H.V. McNeilly 160
John Kroll 320
Edward Krueger 160
Mrs. H. Prochnow 160
Geo. Luther 160
Robert McNeilly 160

30
29 Union Flat
28
27
26
25

Geo. Rafus 88
J.F. Whealen 240
R.T. Whealen
Wm McNeilly
A.D. McNeilly
Robt. McNeilly 160
Mrs. Sam'l. Heth 320
Edward Kroll 160
Thomas A. Sanders 160
F.G. Diercks Baptist Church
F.G. Diercks 160
Mary Lloyd 160

Geo. Rafus
R.T. Whealen 80
Wm McNeilly 160
S.A. McNeilly 305
Robert McNeilly 520
Jas. W. Sanders 120
M. Dyckman 320 C. Fannice Lessee
School Land 160
G.H. Attergott Lessee 160

31
32
33
34
35
36

Chas. Schroder
A.E. Kilroy Wm Krieger Lessee
Geo. Krieger 160
Robt. McNeilly 160
Res. C.J. Ochs 160
G.W. Smith 279.44
Thos. A. Sanders 160
J.J. Kneale 160
E. Kneale 160
M. Kroll Lessee 160

23

Spaniards themselves had never visited. Although small in build, they were remarkable horses, agile and sure-footed. In the 19th century, they were crossed with heavier breeds to produce horses well suited for field work on wheat farms.

PACK HORSES

The first white men to visit the inland Northwest, the Lewis and Clark expedition, found the Indians using horses for both riding and packing.[5] After leaving their river transportation on the Missouri River in what is now Montana, Lewis and Clark used Indian pack horses to carry their possessions, supplies, and equipment until they reached the Clearwater.

Pack horses had wide use before wheeled vehicles entered the area, and after wheeled vehicles were used in country that could accommodate roads, pack animals were still used in the rougher, steeper, and more mountainous areas of the West.

Shortly after Lewis and Clark made their exploration of the Northwest, fur trappers covered most of the area in search of beaver. These men depended on pack horses to move their supplies and transport their pelts. Following the mountain men or fur trappers were the miners, who also needed pack horses to transport their equipment and supplies. After the miners came the cattlemen who used wagons in areas which permitted their use and pack animals in areas which did not.

The homesteader who desired to farm depended primarily on wagons since country which was too rough for their use was also too rough for farming.

When mining first started to boom in southwest Idaho in the 1860s, many large pack strings (75 to 100 head) hauled supplies from Marysville and Sutter's Fort in the Sacramento Valley of California all the way to the diggings at Silver City, Idaho. When the Virginia City, Montana, gold boom was on, pack strings hauled supplies from Lewiston, Idaho, across the Nez

Perce trail that followed the divide between the Clearwater and Salmon Rivers to the gold fields in Virginia City. These were some of the longer hauls. When the Buffalo Hump boom was going, most of the supplies for that area were hauled by pack strings from Grangeville to the Buffalo Hump. High grade ore was often carried out of the mining camps by pack string.

Many unusual items have been packed into mining camps on pack strings. Examples are back bars, pianos, large cook stoves, and all kinds of heavy mining equipment. One mine on the Middle Fork of the Salmon boasted a small steam engine to turn an ore grinder. This steam engine was packed in on a pack string.

For many years, cattle and sheep ranches in the more remote sections of the Salmon, Snake and Imnaha Rivers depended on pack animals for their supplies. Horse-drawn mowers, rakes, and plows have been disassembled and carried by pack animals into remote ranches.

STAGE COACHES

In 1862, a string of big coaches was brought to Washington from California by George H. Thomas, a former president of the California Stage Company. He ran 12 stages between Walla Walla, Washington, and Lewiston, Idaho. Stage service was later extended to Boise, Idaho, by way of the Grande Ronde Valley and Baker City, Oregon.[6]

Southern Idaho was served by a stage line established in 1864 by Ben Holladay. This was a branch of the Overland Stage. It passed from Salt Lake City to Malad, through the valleys of the Raft River and Snake River and into Boise.

In 1871, the Northwestern Stage Company went into operation. It provided service for passengers travelling between Utah and Washington. A traveller from the East might arrive in Utah on the Central Pacific Railroad, continue his journey by stage coach as far as one of the Northwestern Stage's stations on the

Fig. 2 Maps of farms and wheat growers in Whitman County, Washington, during the period 1900 to 1912. My father leased 320 acres in section 22, township 16 north, range 42 east from 1905 to 1917. He purchased 175 acres in section 14, in the same township in 1916. He leased other acreage near these locations at various times. These townships are located in the center of Whitman County which at that time was the richest agricultural county in the United States. Mockonema, St. John, and Lacrosse were the three largest wheat stations in the world during that era. Mockonema is located in section 18 of township 16 north, range 43 east, Washington State. St. John is located northwest of section 6 of township 16 north, range 42 east, and Lacrosse is located west of section 30. The two townships include three streams with rugged steep hills between them: the Palouse River, Rebel Flat Creek, and Union Flat Creek. The Palouse River and Union Flat Creek have rocks and boulders scattered throughout their areas, on the slopes and in the valleys. These two areas had a heavy growth of evergreen trees. Rebel flat was free of trees and rocks.

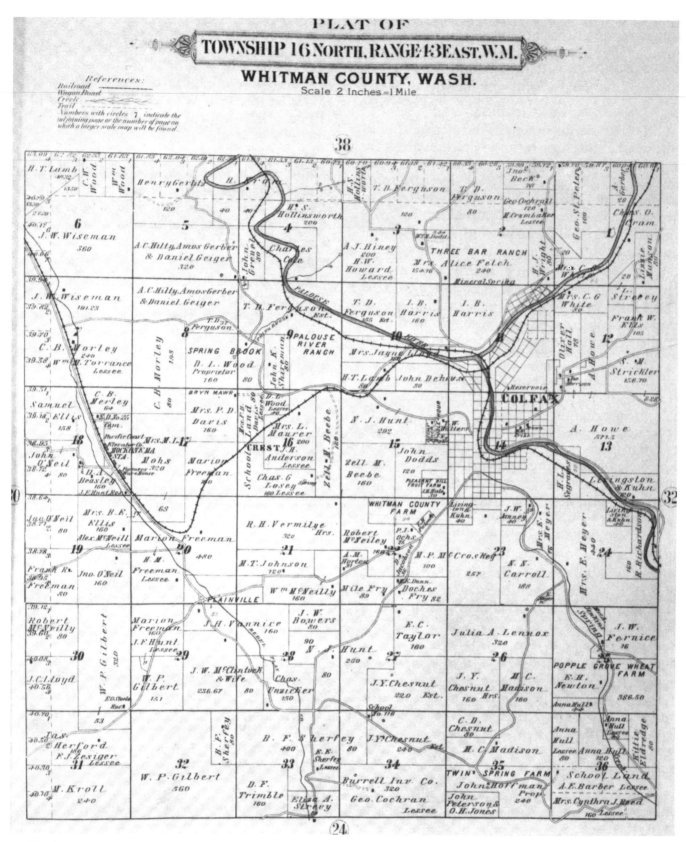

Fig. 3. Map of farms and wheat growers in Whitman County, Washington during the period 1900 to 1912. Courtesy of Herbert W. Ostergen, Colfax, Wash.

Snake River and there board a steamship for the remainder of his journey westward.

Horses used by the stage lines were noted for their stamina and endurance. They were maintained in excellent condition by the stock tenders and blacksmiths employed by the lines. The stations of the stage coach lines, located 12 to 20 miles apart, were reassuring reminders that the frontier had bonds uniting it with the rest of the country. Wherever they travelled, stage drivers brought interesting news and they were eagerly questioned by people in isolated areas.

ORIGINAL HORSES OF THE AREA

Herds of horses were reported to be in possession of Nez Perce, Cayuse, and Palouse Indians as early as 1700. Records show that horses were present in the Palouse area 50 years before appearing in the area of the Dakotas.[7]

Areas west of the Rocky Mountains had an environment that was better adapted to animal survival than areas on the eastern side. The area between the Rocky Mountains and Cascades had deep sheltered canyons as low as 500 feet above sea level with protection from blizzards. Many of these areas furnished winter pasture. Ample forage was available on plateaus in early spring and during summer. Distances from winter to summer pastures ranged within 10 to 100 miles at altitudes of 2-3,000 feet from valley floors. The protecting mountains barred enemy horse thieves as effectually as they warded off winter storms.

These horses weighed from 600 to 1,000 pounds and were 12 to 14 ½ hands in height. They were speedy, intelligent, and hardy. Mixed colors gave them a flashy look at close range and a blend at distances for a natural camouflage. This natural camouflage was a valuable trait in enemy areas.

It is interesting to know that the Nez Perce and Cayuse Indians practiced selective breeding, which consisted chiefly of castrating some of the undesirable stallions and trading the poorer animals to neighboring tribes.

Droves of Indian horses pasturing on public lands were a constant irritation to the early white settlers.[5] These horses were too small to be of any value to the farmer except as saddle ponies. Barbed wire was scarce and costly for fencing purposes and if a farmer kept his animals restricted, he lost the benefits of good pasture near the farm. Some of the farmers were superstitious and believed that crossing the Indian pony with the heavier draft animals produced an offspring of little value.

However, there were situations when many of the wheat farmers were in need of work horses and crossing the Indian pony with the heavy European breeds was a necessity.

THE APPALOOSA BREED

For more than 2,000 years, horsemen have been known to value a breed of spotted horses because of their color markings, speed, endurance, and intelligence. In many places and in various cultures, this breed has been prized highly. These horses have been known by many names. Presently known as the "Appaloosa," the breed derived this name from the soft white wheat area. Here, the Nez Perce Indians were famous for their fine spotted horses.[11]

Mountain men and trappers called this breed the "Nez Perce horse." After the Civil War, homesteaders in the area noticed large herds of horses with odd colored markings and labeled them "Appalousey's." The name stemmed from the Palouse River, a small stream that meanders through the soft white wheat area of eastern Washington. This was a region covered with rich grass in a country of rolling hills. Early fur traders of French Canadian origin called the stream the "Pelouse," which could be translated as "the river with green meadows." However, the Nez Perce Indians had a word "Peluse" — meaning "something sticking out of the water." The Palouse River flows into the Snake River at a point where a big rock embankment exists. The exact origin of the name is, therefore, clouded by uncertainties.

Unfortunately, many of the spotted Indian horses were destroyed by armies sent in to move the Nez Perce tribes to a reservation in 1877. In order to prevent the soldiers from taking their horses, the Indians tried to swim them across the Snake River, during flood stage, from Wallowa Valley, Oregon. Most of the foals drowned. Many horses were killed during the battles of the Nez Perce War while others were confiscated as war loot and moved to Fort Keogh, Montana, where they were sold at auction and scattered to many parts of the U.S.

Over 800 horses belonging to the Spokane Indians were captured in the Battle of Four Lakes within a few miles of Spokane, Washington, on September 8, 1858. Many of the horses were too wild for the army's immediate use. A few horses

Fig. 4. The Mullan Road. Joe Dvorak Photo.

which were considered to be the best ones were selected and the balance were shot on September 9 and 10.[12]

When the first settlers cross-bred these spotted horses with horses of European source, traits of the Appaloosa nearly disappeared. It has been reported that only about 50 Appaloosas with true type, conformation, and color markings of the breed were known to exist in the mid-1930's. Interest in Appaloosa horses was revived in the 1930s during the transition period when wheat farmers were abandoning the horse and adopting the tractor.

NATIVE HORSE FEED

The general environment common to the soft white wheat area was as ideal for horses as it was for wheat production. Native vegetation, soil, seasonal temperatures, precipitation, and wind directions contribute to a natural environment for the horse.

Two varieties of blue bunch wheat grass accounted for 90% of the original vegetation of this area. In extremely dry areas the awned variety (Agropyron spicatum) was the major grass, while in areas with higher soil water storage the awnless variety (Agropyron inerme) prevailed. This variety was prevalent in Whitman county, Washington, and Latah county, Idaho.

If allowed to grow without grazing, it would reach an average height of three feet or better. It was palatable in all stages of growth. According to the present information on the proximate analysis of the bunch grasses and recent information of the nutrient requirement of horses, (Tables 1 and 2) the nutritional status of the horse was without question complete, provided that the reproduction cycle coincided with the seasons of the year. Mares generally foaled in February, March, and April. This provided succulent grass during late pregnancy and lactation. The rich grass of early spring was unusually high in protein, essential minerals, and vitamins. The changing elevations of grazing areas provided a great span of time for succulent feeds. Grass along the breaks of the Snake River and in the areas along the Columbia (known as the Big Bend) supplied new growth as early as January. If the horse moved up the elevations to the high lands, fresh forage was available from January to the middle of June. This provided a big reserve in nutrient storage of the body of the horses. The protein percentage of the grass ranged from 21 to 30%. Maximum requirements of the pregnant and lactating mares ranged from 10 to 14%. Phosphorus needs average about 13% where the contribution of the grass was never lower than 27%.

Young growing foals after weaning and two and three year olds were most likely to suffer nutritional deficiencies. Since there was opportunity to build body reserves of protein, calcium, phosphorus, and vitamins during the spring season, it is doubtful that serious deficiencies among animals ever occurred.

ACQUIRING LAND ON THE FRONTIER

The early wheat farmers acquired their land at a time when governmental policy was directed at making settlement of the frontier attractive to farmers. The railroads had been granted tracts of land along the lines they built — and they were eager to sell this land to new settlers at a nominal price. Other land which had been assigned to the schools could be leased. Finally, for the enterprising homesteader, free land was available for settlement.

Governmental regulations for homesteading were not difficult to meet. The homesteader had

18

Table 1. Nutrient Requirements of Horses.[a]

	Crude Protein %	Calcium grams	%	Phosphorus grams	%
Growing horses					
200 lb.	13.1	11	.40	10	.36
600 lb.	8.0	6	.18	6	.18
800 lb.	7.5	9	.21	9	.21
Mares, last quarter of pregnancy					
600 lb.	9.9	12	.33	11	.30
1,000 lb.	9.7	14	.30	13	.28
1,200 lb.	9.8	18	.30	17	.28
Mares, peak of lactation					
600 lb.	11.2	23	.29	18	.23
1,000 lb.	11.3	30	.29	24	.23
1,200 lb.	11.3	34	.29	27	.23

Table 2. Nutrient composition of blue bunch wheatgrass. Average values of years 1937-38-39-40. Samples taken near 6,000 ft., Dubois, Idaho.[a]

	Total Protein	Calcium grams per day	%	Phosphorus grams per day	%	Ratio of phosphorus to calcium
April, 26	25.4	20.4	.45	15.4	.34	1.3:1
May, 10	20.6	20.9	.46	11.8	.26	1.8:1
May, 25	14.6	19.5	.43	9.1	.20	2.2:1
June, 10	10.3	19.5	.43	7.3	.16	2.7:1
June, 28	7.8	22.0	.48	4.5	.10	4.8:1

Fig. 5. Lewis and Clark Meeting the Flatheads. The Lewis and Clark expedition of 1805-6 was a favorite subject of Charles M. Russell. This scene is rated as one of the greatest of all western historical paintings.

to live on the homestead for five years and make basic improvements. In some areas, he was required to plant trees in order to fulfill the ownership requirements. The original Homestead Act of 1862 limited the homesteader to 160 acres of public land. Legislation passed prior to World War I increased the area of the individual homestead in some cases and reduced the required period of residence from five years to three.

To encourage education, the Morrill Act assigned ownership of sections 16 and 36 of every township to school districts. A settler could lease school land and then request that it be sold. In this way, many settlers gained the opportunity to buy farm land.

MECHANIZATION BEGINS WITH THE REAPER

Traditionally, the harvesting and threshing of grain was slow, tedious work. Hand implements used were the cradle (for harvesting), the flail (for threshing), and the bellows (for winnowing). These tools were used by early settlers of the soft white wheat area. My collection of photos includes a number of harvesting scenes which show the cradle in operation. As for the flail and bellows, their use is demonstrated by two photos

of a Chinese family who resided in Idaho in the first years of this century. (Figs. 8 and 9)

The first wheat grown in the State of Washington was harvested with cradles brought by boat from New York to San Francisco during the 1840s.

Cradles were used to harvest wheat before the reaper. A cradle was a modified scythe, an instrument used for cutting grass or grain plants. A scythe had a long curved blade with a sharp edge attached to the end of a long handle. The cradle consisted of a scythe with long wooden tines attached above and parallel to the blade. These tines were about four inches apart.

Three types of cradles were introduced into the soft white wheat area.[10] They were identified by the shape of their handles. A cradle with a straight handle was identified as the "Turkey Wing"; a cradle with a handle bent inward, upward, and slightly backward was called a "Muley"; and a cradle with a handle bent inward then slightly backward was called a "Grape Vine."

The shape of the handle of the cradle was constructed for the purpose of convenient manipula-

20

Fig. 6. Palouse Falls, the junction of the Palouse region was called the "Peluse" by the French Canadians. Possibly, the name for the Nez Perce horse — Appaloosa — was derived from the French name.

Fig. 7. Bunch grass *(Agropyron inerme).* Courtesy of Lee Sharp

21

Fig. 8. The Flail. The flail was a wooden pole and at its end there was a shorter stick which was hung so as to swing freely. The short stick was called a swiple or swingle. The flail was used to beat the grain to separate the kernels from the heads. Cradled grain was placed on a floor or bare ground and then flailed. Sometimes men or horses trampled the grain to accomplish the separation. Courtesy of Gainford W. Mix.

Fig. 9. The Bellows. The bellows was used to separate the grain from the chaff and straw. The flailed material was pushed over a platform about six feet high, or dropped from a large scoop, while a worker produced wind with the bellows. Courtesy of Gainford W. Mix

tion in cutting a uniform length of the grain plants.

The reaping machine speeded grain harvesting and was an important first step in using the power of horses to replace human labor in the harvest field. The horse-drawn McCormick reaper, patented in 1834, was the first harvesting machine to win wide acceptance. For the pioneer farmer in the Pacific Northwest, ownership of a McCormick reaper was a cherished goal. Farmers went to considerable trouble to obtain reapers. Also much sought after were horse-powered grain threshers.

Ships travelling to the West Coast delivered cargoes of reapers and other machinery. For the Pacific Northwest, the first reaper and the first mowing machine were introduced by George W. Bush in the Puget Sound area in 1856. In the following year, the first thresher was being used on several farms north of the Columbia River. In August 1857, this thresher was reported to be in use on the farm of David J. Chambers, four miles east of Olympia, Washington. The machine threshed 500 bushels of wheat or 800 bushels of oats in a day — or about 10 times the output possible with the old system of trampling grain with horses and winnowing it with the primitive bellows.

The first grain thresher ever brought into eastern Washington made its appearance at the end of the 1861 harvesting season. John A. Simms was the owner. The machine was manufactured at Canton, Ohio, by Aultmann and Taylor and was probably shipped around Cape Horn to San Francisco. Ten horses on a sweep supplied the power to operate the separator.

Seeking to improve the reaper, inventors developed a superior harvesting machine — the self-tying binder. This was the machine that made large-scale wheat farming possible. Some of the binders available in the 1870s tied bundles of grain with wire, while others used twine. Because farmers preferred the twine binders, the wire binders disappeared from the scene before long.

In the history of farm mechanization, the farmers' eager acceptance of the reaper and the binder was of landmark significance because it stimulated further invention and development.

Wherever farmers became aware of the advantages of the new harvesting machines, they wanted them — and they also wanted to purchase or hire threshers. Northwest farmers shared in this generalized enthusiasm for machines that would make grain farming more efficient. However, while grain farmers in other sections of the country found the binder-thresher combination quite sufficient for their needs for many years, wheat farmers of the Northwest were receptive to other innovations. They accepted the header and the early-day combines. For them, mechanization of wheat harvesting had to be a progressive, ongoing development. The Northwest farmers' strong urge to mechanize speeded technological progress in the area's agriculture, as I will show in my forthcoming discussions.

(Figs. 10-34 present a series of pictures depicting early mowing machines, etc.)

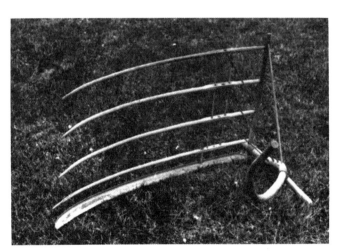

Fig. 10. A Muley Cradle.

Fig. 11. Harvesting wheat with a grape vine cradle. The crooked handle of the "grape vine" cradle made it convenient for the worker to get a longer and wider swath. Courtesy of Caterpiller Tractor Co.

Fig. 12. Tying bundles with stalks of the wheat plant. Cradled wheat was tied into bundles with two small bunches of wheat stalks. The ends of the stalks were twisted together, forming a band around the bundle. The worker on the left was holding a "turkey wing" cradle. Courtesy of Gainford W. Mix.

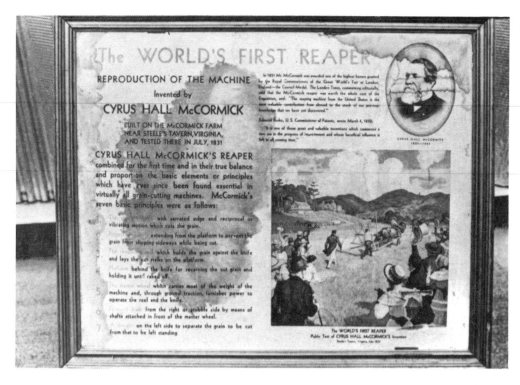

Fig. 13. McCormick reaper and seven basic principles. In 1851 McCormick was awarded one of the highest honors granted by the Royal Commissioners of the Great World's Fair at London, England — the Council Medal. The London Times, commenting editorially, said the McCormick reaper was worth the whole cost of the Exposition. The newspaper added: "The reaping machine from the United States is the most valuable contribution from abroad to the stock of our previous knowledge that we have yet discovered."

Edmund Burk, U.S. Commissioner of Patents, wrote March 4, 1850: "It is one of those great and valuable inventions which commence a new era in the progress of improvement and whose beneficial influence is felt in all coming time."

McCormick's seven basic principles were as follows:

— The straight knife with severed edge and reciprocal or vibrating motion.

— Fingers or guards extending from the platform to prevent the grain from slipping side-ways while being cut.

— The revolving reel, which holds the grain against the knife and lays the cut stalks on the platform.

— Platform behind the knife for receiving the cut grain and holding until raked off.

— The master wheel, which carries most of the weight of the machine and, through ground traction, furnishes power to operate the reel and the knife.

— Forward draft from the right or the stubble side by means of shafts attached in front of the master wheel.

— A divider on the left side to separate the grain to be cut from that to be left standing.

26

Fig. 14. An original McCormick reaper. This machine was shipped around Cape Horn to San Francisco. then by boat up the Snake River to Lewiston, Idaho. It is in the Lion's Club Museum, Cottonwood, Idaho. Joe Dvorak Photo, 1971

Fig. 15. The first public trial of the McCormick reaper. The first public trial of the revolutionary reaper took place in July, 1831. The historic field was near Steele's Tavern, close to Walnut Grove, Virginia. Doubtful neighbors were watching as the machine cut its first swath. While young McCormick walked behind his machine a Negro servant named Jo Anderson raked the platform clear of the cut grain. Courtesy of International Harvester Co.

Fig. 16. The improved reaper. The improved reaper was the model used to harvest grain before the development of the self-binder. Unlike the original McCormick reaper, this was a self-rake reaper. However, binding was still done by hand by workers who followed the machine and gathered up the bundles of cut plants and tied them with stalks of the grain. This machine is on display in the Lion's Club Museum, Cottonwood, Idaho. Joe Dvorak Photocopy

Fig. 17. A reaper owned by Albert Klein in operation in 1908. This improved reaper differed from the original McCormick machine in that it had a sickle similar to that of a modern mower and a reel that would slide a bunch of cut stalks over the rear of the platform. The reel was made of slats with steel tines on the lower edge. The reel slats with tines functioned as a sweeper by passing over the platform surface to the rear of the sickle. Bundles of the plants were dropped behind the reaper where they were picked up and tied with the stalks of the grain. Courtesy of Albert Klein, Edwall, Washington

Fig. 18. The 1908 reaper in operation in 1968.
Courtesy of Albert Klein

Fig. 19. Lever hay baling press. An early hay baler, powered by one or two horses. This press required one man to feed the baler and another to tie the bales.

This illustration and other engravings of horse-powered hay machinery were presented in a book entitled, The American Farmer, edited by Charles Flint, secretary of the State Board of Agriculture of Massachusetts, and published in 1884 by Ralph H. Park and Company. A copy of this book is at present the property of Lawrence M. Welle, Uniontown, Washington. The engravings were photographed by Joe Dvorak. The hay equipment is similar to that used in the soft white wheat area. Courtesy of Lawrence Wells, Joe Dvorak photo

Fig. 20. Farguhar's thresher and cleaner. Geared for work with power, elevator and straw-stacker attachment. Courtesy of Lawrence M. Weele, Joe Dvorak photocopy

Fig. 21. Baling press by steam power. Courtesy of Lawrence M. Welle, Joe Dvorak photocopy

Fig. 22. The McCormick iron mower. Courtesy of Lawrence Welle, Joe Dvorak photocopy

Fig. 23. New Buckeye Mower. Courtesy of Lawrence M. Welle, Joe Dvorak photocopy

Fig. 24. New Buckeye table-rake and adjustable reel. Courtesy of Lawrence W. Welle, Joe Dvorak photocopy

Fig. 25. The Thomas sulky rake. Courtesy of Lawrence W. Welle, Joe Dvorak photocopy

Fig. 26. The gleaner hay and grain rake. Courtesy of Lawrence W. Welle, Joe Dvorak photocopy

Fig. 27. Hay making with horse equipment. This is a hay rake, generally referred to as a dump rake. It was used to winnow mowed hay after a short period of cutting in the sun. After the hay was raked into windrows, men made haycocks for further curing before the hay was stored in haymows or stacks. The harnesses of the horses were fitted tight and snug with heavy breeches. This was necessary to control the operation of the rake. Courtesy of Dave Ferguson, Clarkston, Washington

Fig. 28. One-horse dump rake. These hay rakes were sometimes called sulky rakes. Courtesy of Joe Dvorak

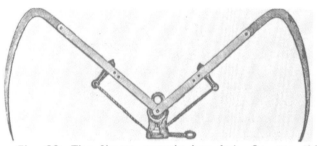

Fig. 29. The Noyes grapple hay fork. Courtesy of Lawrence W. Welle, Joe Dvorak photocopy

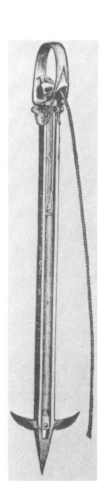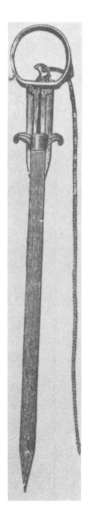

Fig. 20. Harpoon hay fork. Courtesy of Lawrence Welle, Joe Dvorak photocopy

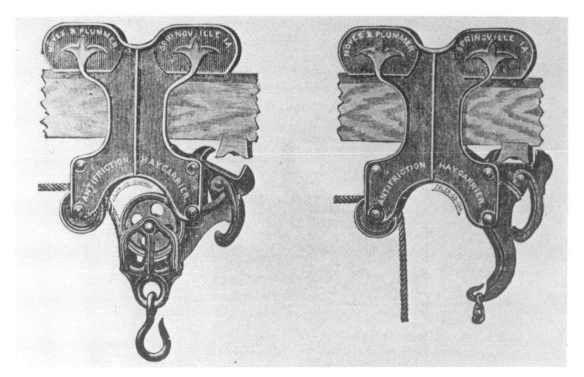

Fig. 31. Carrier for unloading and stacking hay. The 1884 farming handbook explained the operation of the hay fork carrier: "The cut at the left shows the carrier just after the pulley, to which the fork is attached, has run up on to the crooked arm on which it rides. The carrier is now detached from the lug on the track, and had commenced to move off. On returning, the catch strikes the lug, the crooked arm is released, and the fork returns to the load." Courtesy of Lawrence M. Welle, Joe Dvorak photocopy

Fig. 32. Noyes field pitching apparatus. Method used to stack hay with a grapple fork during the 1880s. Courtesy of Lawrence M. Welle

Fig. 33. Oxen ready for work. Many of the first plow teams were oxen. Courtesy of Mel Taggart

Fig. 34. Horse-powered ferry boat. This horse-powered ferry boat was built by Abe Carter and his brother on the banks of the Columbia River at the mouth of Crab Creek. They built it to ferry their sheep back and forth across the river. Power came from horses walking around and around the boat deck harnessed to a capstan, which set paddle wheels in motion. Since this horse-powered ferry was used at White Bluffs, it was called "The White Bluffs Ferry." In 1900, it was sold to George Borden of White Bluffs. Borden propelled the boat daily with two horses called Pete and Ginger. They moved sheep, cattle, horses and wagons and rigs. The White Bluffs Ferry handled the traffic from Yakima to Spokane. In 1904, a large barge at Trinidad broke loose and floated to White Bluffs. The task of returning the barge to Trinidad was so difficult that the owner sold it to Borden, and Borden fastened the barge behind the horse ferry when needed for increased service. Courtesy of Robert H. Ruby

Part Two
THE WHEAT HORSE

The general characteristics required of a horse to be used for wheat production in the soft white wheat area of the Pacific Northwest were determined by the fact that the environmental situation favored the use of multiple-horse hitches in areas of steep sloping hills with soft footings.

The horses which worked most satisfactorily in the multiple-hitch arrangements were of medium size. About 1,450 pounds was considered to be the ideal weight of a wheat horse. Heavier horses were useful for draft purposes — as in logging, freighting, and construction work. Those heavier horses, if hitched closely together, would be cramped and clumsy; they would have been difficult to control on hillsides and almost impossible to guide smoothly in turning. The larger multiple-hitch teams used for combine harvesting — consisting of 16 to 44 horses — would not have been practical without the availability of mules and medium size horses.

In the process of working with big teams, the Northwest wheat farmers became expert teamsters. Multiple-hitching of large teams came to be used not only in plowing but also in harrowing, seed-drilling, and harvesting. The farmers recognized that certain horses performed well in certain positions and they were careful to place their best horses in key positions — such as in the plow furrow, next to wagon tongue, in the lead position for teams with horses hitched in tandem or any other position where the line was required.

A six-horse team was used to pull a two-bottom, 14-inch gang plow in areas of steep slopes similar to those of Whitman and Walla Walla counties of eastern Washington. An eight-horse team was used to pull an 18-inch, two-bottom gang plow and a 14-inch, three-bottom gang plow. The six-horse team would plow an average of four acres per day with the two-bottom, 14-inch plow. The eight-horse team with the two-bottom, 18-inch plow would plow an average of five acres per day and six acres with the three-bottom, 14-inch gang plow.

The 16-horse team would plow an average of 18 acres per day with a four-bottom, 14-inch gang plow on the level areas of Adams county.

Four horse teams were used to pull an 8-foot seed-drill. Six horses were required to pull a 10-foot seed-drill. The 8-foot drill would seed 18 to 20 acres per day as compared to 25 acres for the 10-foot.

Six horses hitched abreast were used to pull a four section, 24-foot drag harrow which would pulverize 35 acres per day.

Many stallions and mares of European breeds were imported into the soft white wheat area during the 1880s and 1890s but the offspring of these were too heavy for the multiple-hitch teams.

The Cleveland Bays were ideal horses for this area since their weight averaged 1,350 to 1,500 pounds.

Apparently, other sources of horses were more convenient from the standpoint of time, cost, and adaptability. The Cleveland Bays were not used to any great extent.

A common practice was to build a corral around a source of water with the top rails high enough to prevent a Thoroughbred, Clydesdale, or Hambletonian stallion from jumping over the fence and the Indian mare could creep under the lower rail. A Thoroughbred or Hambletonian stallion was placed in the corral to breed the mares of the Indian ponies. This mating produced a mare weighing between 1,000 and 1,100 pounds. After a period of three or four years, a Clydesdale stallion was placed in these corrals. The offspring from the Clydesdale stallion and the mare of the first cross gave a horse weighing an average of 1,350 pounds. This explained the reason for the large number of farm horses with white faces and white stockings during the era of the horse interlude.

THE WHEAT HORSE RATION
For the horse used in the production of wheat, the feeds available included oats, wheat, barley, wheat hay, and wheat straw.

Steamed-rolled oats were preferred over barley or wheat because they could be fed under all conditions of heavy or light work without the danger of founder or any digestive disturbances. Barley was always available and was generally a cheaper source of grain than oats or wheat. It was fed in

Fig. 35. A typical wheat horse. This was a 1,600 pound mare owned by A. N. Keith in 1910. This mare was of the type used in key positions of the Soft White Wheat Area terms. These key positions were in the plow furrow, leaders for teams with horses hitched in tandem, horses used next to the wagon tongue, or any position where the line was required. I am the exhibitor. Bertha Anderson Stipe Photo, 1910

Fig. 36. Three 8-horse plow teams, 1919. These three 8-horse teams are resting after a long pull up a steep slope. Each team is hitched to a 2-bottom, 18-inch gang plow. I am the driver of the center team. It required about five hours — a full half day — to complete one trip around the area being plowed. The rate of travel averaged about 1.5 miles per hour. The three teams would plow approximately 16 acres per day. A 6-horse team hitched abreast was the most common of the field teams for plows, drills and cultivators (discs, weeders and harrows). Teams of four, five and six were hitched abreast for harrows and weeders. Six-horse teams had the greatest number to be hitched abreast. Teams of plows with six, seven or eight horses abreast would have one, two and three horses, respectively, in the plowed ground. For this reason, teams of more than eight horses were hitched in tandem. Eight horses were hitched in tandem of fours to plows. Plows that required 10 horses were hitched in tandem of fives or six in the rear and four in the lead. In the level farm areas of central Washington, four horses or mules would be able to pull the same load that took six in the hilly areas similar to that of Whitman and Walla Walla counties. Horses for these teams weighed from 1,300 to 1,500 pounds. On soft underfooting or on steep hills, heavier horses could not withstand the crowded conditions required for multi-horse hitches.

the steam-rolled or ground form. Wheat was fed steam-rolled, ground, or whole. The incidence of digestive disturbances was greater with horses fed wheat.

The most common roughage was wheat hay. This was the wheat plant cut when the grain was in the early dough stage. This gave a roughage high in soluble carbohydrate with a high level of energy. It was not an uncommon practice for the farmer to plant a special variety of barley or wheat to be used specifically for hay. Another common grain used for hay was an awnless variety of barley, referred to as "Bald Barley." However, the greater portions of the hay came from the regular wheat crop. This hay came from the corners of the fields and the area where the first swaths were to be cut with header or combine. If these areas were not cut for hay, they were generally lost from trampling.

Limited quantities of alfalfa hay were grown. Alfalfa was not fed in large quantities to horses assigned to heavy work. Since it was high in protein (12 to 16%), it produced stress on the kidneys, especially if stall fed. It was an excellent feed for horses being wintered outside of the barn.

This type of feeding was unique to the soft white wheat area of the Pacific Northwest. Farmers fed what was available, with oats and timothy being the standard feed in some parts of the county, corn in others.

For a summer pasture, the seed of a winter wheat variety was planted in the spring — March or April. Winter wheat varieties planted in the spring would not mature, but made a heavy growth and clustered close to the ground. Redtop, bromegrass, and Kentucky bluegrass grew freely in low areas next to streams.

During the early days of wheat farming, there were areas of bunch grass available for pasture. After a summer or winter on bunch grass, the horse was ready for work. He did not fatigue easily or shrink in weight. Wheat was the most common hay fed to working horses. Wheat straw was the standard winter feed.

After the fall work was finished or after the ground was frozen, the horses were turned into a field of wheat stubble where wheat heads were available for feed until snow covered the ground. Straw from stacks was the main source of food throughout the winter. Considerable grain was carried through the separator in the straw stacks during threshing, which was available for feed.

As soon as the snow melted and the temperature began to rise in late February and early March, the horses would leave the straw stacks for fresh plant growth. If left in the fields, horses would lose body weight. If they were to be used for early spring work, they were placed in the barn and fed a light ration of grain and hay until farm work began.

DISEASES OF THE HORSE

Diseases of horses of the soft white wheat area from 1850 to the early 1920s were mostly non-infectious. Most of the health problems of horses were due to man's ignorance and carelessness in management.

Founder (Laminitis), azutoria (hemoglobinuria), heaves, and impactions of the intestional tract occurred more frequently than any other types of illness.

Founder was a major problem during harvesting, especially in extremely hot weather. Inexperienced teamsters were a contributing factor. Founder could be caused from drinking too much water after the horse was overworked during an extremely hot afternoon. Within an hour after the evening watering, the horse would be too stiff to walk. This could have been prevented if the horse had been allowed only about three swallows, then rested for a couple of hours before watering.

As soon as the conditions of founder were discovered, the horse was left standing in a stream of cold running water until able to walk without severe pain. In acute cases, the hooves would slip. Six months or a year were required for recovery. Wheat grain founder was less severe. With a modified diet, the horse would recover in a few days.

Azutoria was a condition directly connected with the consumption of a high level of feed during a period of idleness. The disease was never observed at pasture or with constant daily work. It was most prevalent during the middle of the work season when a heavy rain restricted the horses to their stalls. After a couple of days of standing and eating a full ration, a half hour of work brought on lameness and perspiration, along with general trembling and swelling of the muscles. Pulse and breathing were accelerated and urine, if passed, was highly colored dark

Fig. 37. Front view of an 8-horse plow team. Here is the front view of the rear team in the preceding photo. These are 1,400-pound horses, each pulling the same share of the load. The gee (right) horse of each 4-horse team walks in the plow furrow. Four lines on the outside horses of each 4-horse team are used for driving.

Fig. 38. Three 8-horse teams were being hitched to plows. After breakfast, the horses were untied from the mangers and turned loose to drink at their convenience. Then they were hitched for the day's work. The picture shows drivers placing each horse in its assigned position.

Fig. 39. Seven 6-horse plow teams. Seven 6-horse teams are shown, each of them hitched to a 2-bottom 14-inch gang plow. Each team is hitched in tandem of threes. These teams are plowing land owned by G. B. Mix about one mile northwest of Moscow, Idaho. The seven teams would plow a total average of 30 acres per day. Hodgins Drug Photo, 1928

Fig. 40. Seven-drill and five-harrow teams. The six 8-foot drills (seeders) were pulled by four mules each and the 10-foot drill was pulled by six mules. The 8-foot drills averaged approximately 16 acres each per day. The seven drills averaged approximately 116 acres per day. Five 25-foot harrows pulled by six mules each or a total of 30 mules cultivated an average of 200 acres per day. Five saddle horses were used by the drivers of the harrow teams. Four horses were used to pull the seed wagons. A total of 69 horses and mules were used to plant this crop in a level area. This picture is on display in Pioneer Village of Fort Walla Walla Park. Ross Watson Photo, 1971

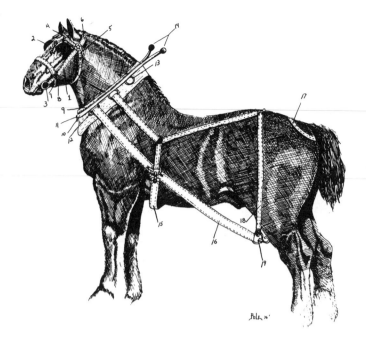

Fig. 41. A popular harness for big teams. A typical harness used on horses or mules of the multiple horse teams of the soft white wheat area.

1. Halter bridle
2. Bridle blind (wing type)
3. Bridle bit
4. Brow band
5. Throat latch
6. Crown piece
7. Halter chin strap
8. Ring for lead chain or rope
9. Collar
10. Hames
11. Hame strap
12. Ring for breast strap
13. Ring for lines
14. Hame knobs
15. Belly Band
16. Tug or trace
17. Crupper
18. Hip strap
19. Butt chain hook

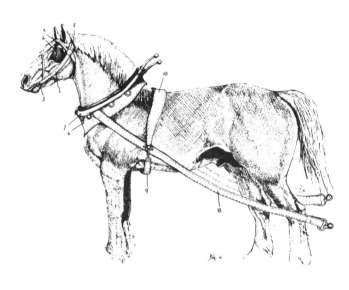

Fig. 42. Common tug harness. This was a popular harness for horses or mules not used in key positions on multiple-horse teams.

1. Bridle
2. Bridle blind (cup type)
3. Bridle bit
4. Brow band
5. Crown piece
6. Collar
7. Hames
8. Leather tug or trace
9. Belly band
10. Back band
11. Single tree hook

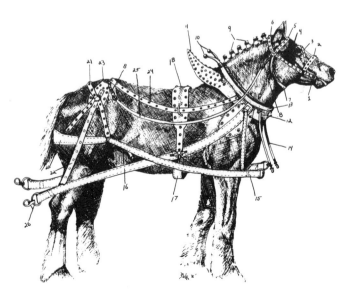

Fig. 43. Harness for show purposes. Harness used on a wheel team for 4-, 6- and 8-in-hand of a circus or any team used for exhibition purposes.

1. Bridle bit
2. Nose piece
3. Face piece
4. Blinds
5. Brow band
6. Crown band
7. Throat latch
8. Celluloid ring spreader
9. Rosettes braided in the mane
10. Hame knobs
11. Hame and collar housing
12. Collar
13. Hames
14. Breast strap
15. Spreader strap
16. Tug or trace
17. Pole strap
18. Back band
19. Lead rein
20. Buttock breeching
21. Hip breeching
22. Tug strap
23. Ring for attachment of tug, breeching and hame straps
24. Backstrap for breeching and hame
25. Lead strap
26. Hook for butt chains.

42

brown, red, or black. This disease was often called "black water" or "Monday morning disease."

The general treatment was fasting for horses kept in the stall. Another treatment was to pasture on grass for about 10 days. The most successful method of preventing azutoria was to feed wheat bran instead of the regular grain ration during the period of inactivity.

Heaves were generally the result of a lung injury; horses with heaves were sometimes referred to as being "wind broken." The cause was usually overexertion under hot, dusty conditions. Horses with heaves breathed with a wheezing noise.

Impactions were common during winter months, when horses were allowed to rely on wheat straw for their entire diet. If sufficient salt and water were made available, this condition was prevented.

Colic resulted most commonly from eating unlimited quantities of new wheat kernels or heads, which produced excessive gas in the digestive system. In acute cases, the horse would rise on his hind feet and fall backwards, causing ruptures of internal organs or injury to the brain.

Very few infectious diseases appeared among horses in this area until the 1920s. Then distemper became common among horses in the town delivery barns and glanders prevailed among horses used for logging.

Veterinarians were seldom requested to treat cattle, sheep, pigs, or dogs. However, bloat and milk fever were common diseases of cattle. Hog cholera did not appear in the area until the early 1920s. Rinds of hams fed in garbage to pigs at Walla Walla, Washington, introduced cholera to the area. These hams were shipped to Walla Walla from the corn belt.

HARNESSES OF THE WHEAT HORSE

The first harnesses used on the horse for wheat production were makeshift types. All sorts of materials were used — such as odd pieces of leather, chains of various sizes and lengths, gunny sacks, and hay wire. Gunny sacks were wrapped around hames because collars were not available. Some equipment and harnesses were available from stage lines and freight wagon outfits.

The first harness makers of the area made a simple leather tug harness. This included leather collars, steel reinforced wooden hames, and leather tugs with leather back band and leather belly band. Most of the early harnesses had only bridles, collars, hames, and trace chains with belly bands. The trace chains were wrapped in crude, thin leather tubes to avoid blemishing the sides and hind legs of the horses.

The most practical type of harness used after 1910 was the "butt chain harness." Its tugs were made of leather from hame to the hocks of the horses and chains from the hocks to the single trees. These harnesses were strong, not likely to be torn apart, and were efficient for the teamster's hitching and unhitching. This harness was composed of a bridle, set of hames, tugs, belly band, hip straps, and crupper with straps to the attachment of the belly band.

GLOSSARY

Harness — combination of leather pieces and metals that connect an animal to a carriage, wagon, plow, etc. Harness equipment for a horse or mule includes bridle, collar, hames, tugs or traces, back band, belly band, and breeching.

Bridle — used to control the animal. A bridle is made up of headstall, bit, reins, blinds, throatlatch, noseband, chinstrap, and browband. The headstall includes browband, crownpiece, blinds, facepiece, and throatlatch.

Collar — leather pad that fits snugly on the horse's shoulder for the attachment of the hames. It bears the weight of loads pulled.

Hames — two curved wood and metal pieces that fit on the collar. Leather, tugs or trace chains are attached to the hames.

Tugs or Traces — long leather straps that connect the collar to the single tree. (Chains were used instead of leather during the pioneer days.) Some tugs were made of leather with short chains hooked to the leather tug near the hocks of the horse. These were referred to as the "butt chain harness". Butt chain harnesses were the most common kind used throughout the soft white wheat area.

Back band — leather strap that passes over the back of the horse to hold the tugs in place.

Belly band — wide leather strap that passes under the horse just to the rear of the fore flank to keep the tugs in place and to prevent the collar from choking the horse.

Crupper — Leather loop that passes under the horse's tail and is fastened to the back band or to the tugs by two straps from the top of the rump

43

Fig. 44. Harness for wheel teams of wagons built to haul light loads pulled by horses weighing 1200 to 1400 pounds. The breeching is attached to the crupper and fits over the rump instead of buttocks.

1. Bridle
2. Bridle bit
3. Bridle blinds (cup)
4. Face straps
5. Crown band
6. Throatlatch
7. Hame knobs
8. Collar
9. Hames
10. Breast strap
11. Pole strap
12. Belly band
13. Tug or trace
14. Butt chain hook
15. Hip strap
16. Crupper
17. Breeching
18. Ring for connecting crupper and breeching to hip and hame straps
19. Tug strap
20. Hame strap

Fig. 45. Harness for a single horse buggy or cart. Harness designed for a horse to be hitched between shafts of a buggy.

1. Bridle bit
2. Face piece
3. Bridle blind (cup)
4. Brow band
5. Crown piece
6. Throat latch
7. Check rein
8. Terret
9. Neck strap
10. Breast collar
11. Back band
12. Belly band
13. Shaft Loop
14. Tug or trace
15. Reins or lines
16. Crupper
17. Breeching
18. Loop for breeching strap
19. Hip strap
20. Single tree hook

to each tug at back band attachment; helps keep the tugs in place.

Breeching — part of the harness that passes around the buttocks of the horse. Its main purpose is to control the forward motion of a vehicle on down grades and to use the horse to back a wheeled implement. It is attached to the hames, tugs, and pole strap.

Throatlatch — a strap which passes under a horse's throat and helps to keep a bridle or halter in place.

Polestrap — heavy leather strap that passes over the belly band under the chest and breast of the horse, attaching the breeching to the neck yoke. It is held in place by a collar strap.

THE HORSE COLLAR AND ITS CONTRIBUTION

The horse collar was invented by the Chinese as early as 300 A.D.[1] It was widely used in Europe for centuries before settlers brought it to America in the 1600s. It was soon learned that the collar was not adaptable to the ox because of the formation of the neck and shoulders.

The ox was slow and the split hooves made the use of shoes impracticable. The horse could pull five times more weight than the ox and at a greater speed. The horse's superiority was enhanced by the use of the horse collar.

The horse and collar contributed to the development of every industry and distribution system, making production and transportation

more efficient. The horse collar enabled horses and mules to plow fields, cultivate crops, reap the harvest, and haul it to a place of storage or processing.

The horse collar, although less widely acclaimed than the steam engine, ranks among the major inventions responsible for the phenomenal growth of America during the 18th and 19th centuries.

HORSE VISION — WHY BRIDLE BLINDS

Horsemen learned through experience that the vision of a horse should be controlled under certain situations. Man controls a horse's vision with the attachment of a cup-shaped piece of leather on the bridle just to the rear of the eyes, called bridle blinds.

The anatomical structure of the horse's head and neck and the location of his eyes make it essential to use blinds in certain situations where strange movements and noises may occur on the side or rear of a team. A horse can see objects on each side of his head and body at the same time. In other words, he has monocular vision. He cannot focus both eyes on an object which is four to six feet in front of him.

Actually, the horse cannot see the feed he eats because of the location of his eyes and the shape of his head. To investigate objects nearby and on the ground, he lowers his head. He locates feed by feeler hairs on his lips and nostrils. Even if he lowers his head, he cannot see the grass near his mouth. He selects grass with his feelers and his sense of smell.

Blinds were never used on saddle horses. A cow pony would not be able to perform efficiently with blinds because he must see objects at all times while turning and moving at irregular speeds.

Blinds were (and are) sometimes used on race horses. Some race horses have difficulty following the contour of the tract, which causes stumbling. This tendency to stumble in a sulky or saddle race could be remedied by having the cup-shaped blind placed under the horse's eyes. This forces a horse to lift his knees, thus eliminating the possibility of stumbling.

Blinds were usually used on plow, wheat drill, and harrow teams in the soft white wheat area. These teams consisted of six and eight horses. Road teams pulling buggies and wheat wagon teams hitched in tandem were also driven with blinds. Tumble weeds, automobiles, or animals running about often disturbed a team, especially if these movements were in the rear. Horses were especially afraid of the noisy, fast-moving automobile.

However, the bridle blind had its disadvantages. Many incidents occurred where a horse would see an object moving toward him from a side view. Then it disappeared out of sight to the rear, although the horse could still hear sounds. Sometimes, the puzzled horse would become frightened and try to run away to escape possible danger.

On one occasion, every horse in a combine team of 22 horses became punchy. A colt came

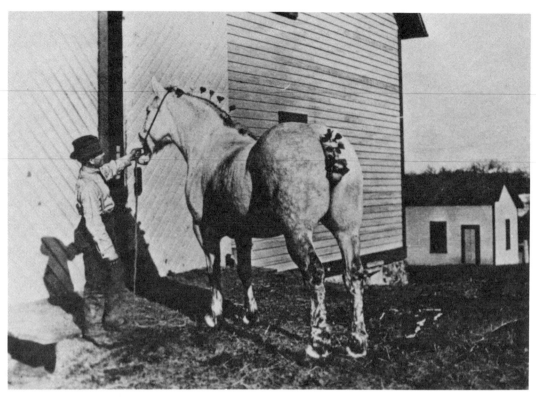

Fig. 47. A Percheron mare. The grand champion Percheron mare of the International Livestock Show, Chicago, Illinois, 1910. This mare was purchased by the University of Idaho, Moscow. She weighed 1800 pounds. Hodgins Drug Store Photo, 1913

Fig. 48. Purebred Clydesdale and Percheron mares. The white-faced mare on the left is a Clydesdale. The dapple grey is a Percheron. These were owned by the University of Idaho, Moscow.

galloping through unharvested wheat on the gee and rear side of the team and frightened every horse. When every horse in a team of 22 becomes scared and starts to move rapidly at the same time, the driver has an alarming situation on his hands!

Many big teams were driven without bridle blinds during the era of horse-operated machinery for wheat production in the soft white wheat area. Some teamsters questioned the need for the use of blinds and teams driven without blinds usually appeared to be as easily handled and as docile as teams that wore them.

THE MULE AND WHEAT FARMING

The mule was an ideal work animal in the big team hitches of the Palouse hills and the surrounding areas of eastern Washington during the early days of wheat farming.[2] He was better adapted to the rugged operations of producing wheat on a rugged, hilly terrain than was the horse. He was especially adapted to operations where more than 30 work animals were required for a farm unit. Therefore, a farmer of 160 to 400 acres requiring only 15 to 20 work animals generally preferred to use horses.

The term "mule" is applied to the offspring of a cross between the *EQUUS CABALLUS* and the *E. ASINUS* species. There are two kinds of hybrids: (1) the mule proper, which is the offspring of a jack ass and a mare *(EQUUS CABALLUS)*, and (2) the hinny, which is the offspring of the stallion and the female ass or jennet. The hinny is more refined in his physical characteristics than the mule. His ears are smaller and similar to those of the horse. He lacks the physical ruggedness of the mule. Little attention was directed to the breeding of this hybrid in the soft white wheat area or more other sections of the U.S. Hinnies were produced for light work in Spain, New Mexico, and sections of South America.

The wheat rancher learned from experience that it was not practical to mix horses and mules on hitches of big teams unless there were insufficient numbers of either available to complete a team of all horses or all mules. Also, it was not advisable to hitch mules to machinery when the rate of travel was regulated by horses or to use mules to regulate the speed of horses. For example, if mules were used for pulling header wagons, while horses were used to push the header, there would be a conflict in the rate of travel which would tire both teamsters and the work animals, resulting in an inefficient operation.

The mules traveled at a slower and a more uniform pace on level terrain and up-grade than the horses did. Sometimes the rate of travel was so slow that the machinery failed to function properly. This was especially true of the ground-powered combine harvester. The mule moved faster down-grade than the horse. His rate would reach as much as three miles per hour on long steep slopes. He had the tendency to squat and dart.

On the other hand, the horses traveled at an irregular pace when drawing machinery upgrade. If they were not carefully controlled by the driver, they tended to move in alternate jerks. Occasionally some would lunge while others would almost stop. Driving upgrade required an experienced teamster who understood the situation and had the ability to correct it.

The horse had difficulty walking downgrade, especially if the terrain was extremely steep. Because he had difficulty flexing his hind legs, the horse would constantly attempt to walk sideways while going downgrade. This resulted in a much slower rate of travel than that of the mule. This also caused the header portion of the combine to "bobble" in and out of the uncut grain. All of this resulted in a reduction in the acres cut in a day.

Contrast in the performance of the horse and the mule was undoubtedly due to an anatomical difference which some anatomist should endeavor to explain.

Mules were more easily handled as a header team than horses. One of the reasons the mules were adaptable to the combine harvester was their ability to walk sideways. Since the header was pushed instead of pulled, it was necessary to turn the machinery as a man would propel a wheelbarrow. If the turn were toward the right, the left team of four mules moved forward to the left, against the beam of the header. This required side-stepping in which there was the tendency of the mules to step on the tops of the hoofs of the one to his left. This caused injuries. Mules are at a disadvantage when they are required to pull machinery in areas of soft dirt. They tire more easily than horses.

The mule seems to be able to know when it is time to be unhitched. When a team of mules reaches the area of the field at which they are generally unhitched, they will use every scheme possible to get their master to stop for the day.

It was never necessary for the teamster to be careful to avoid over-exerting a team of mules under strenuous conditions in an environment of high temperatures. When they become tired they moved at a slower rate or would automatically stop for a rest.

Mules would not drink an excessive quantity of water after being overheated, nor would they overeat if they had access to more than their regular allowance of food. Both situations would cause founder in the horse.

Where it was necessary to use hired teamsters of all types, especially men who were not especially interested in the best care of the work animal, the mule was better adapted than the horse. The mule could not be overworked and did not require the special care of the horse.

(The following pages present an album of work horses at work and in exhibition, as well as farming equipment and facilities.)

Fig. 49. Typical Clydesdale and Percheron mares. These were owned by the University of Idaho, Moscow. Hodgins Drug Store Photo

Fig. 50. Percheron and Clydesdale mares at the Lewiston Horse Show, Lewiston, Idaho, 1914.

Fig. 51. 6-in-hand show team. This team was owned by the University of Idaho, Moscow, and was part of the Little International parade. Wagon teams of 6-in-hand were driven with six lines. These horses weighed 1600 to 1800 pounds and were too heavy for pulling machinery in the fields. Courtesy of Lester Kimberling.

Fig. 52. Three wheat-seeding outfits. One 6-horse and two 4-horse drills shown seeding wheat on George Nelson's farm near Krupp, Washington, October 15, 1909. A 4-horse neck-yoke was used, since there was considerable weight on the tongue of the drill. Courtesy of Richard Walter

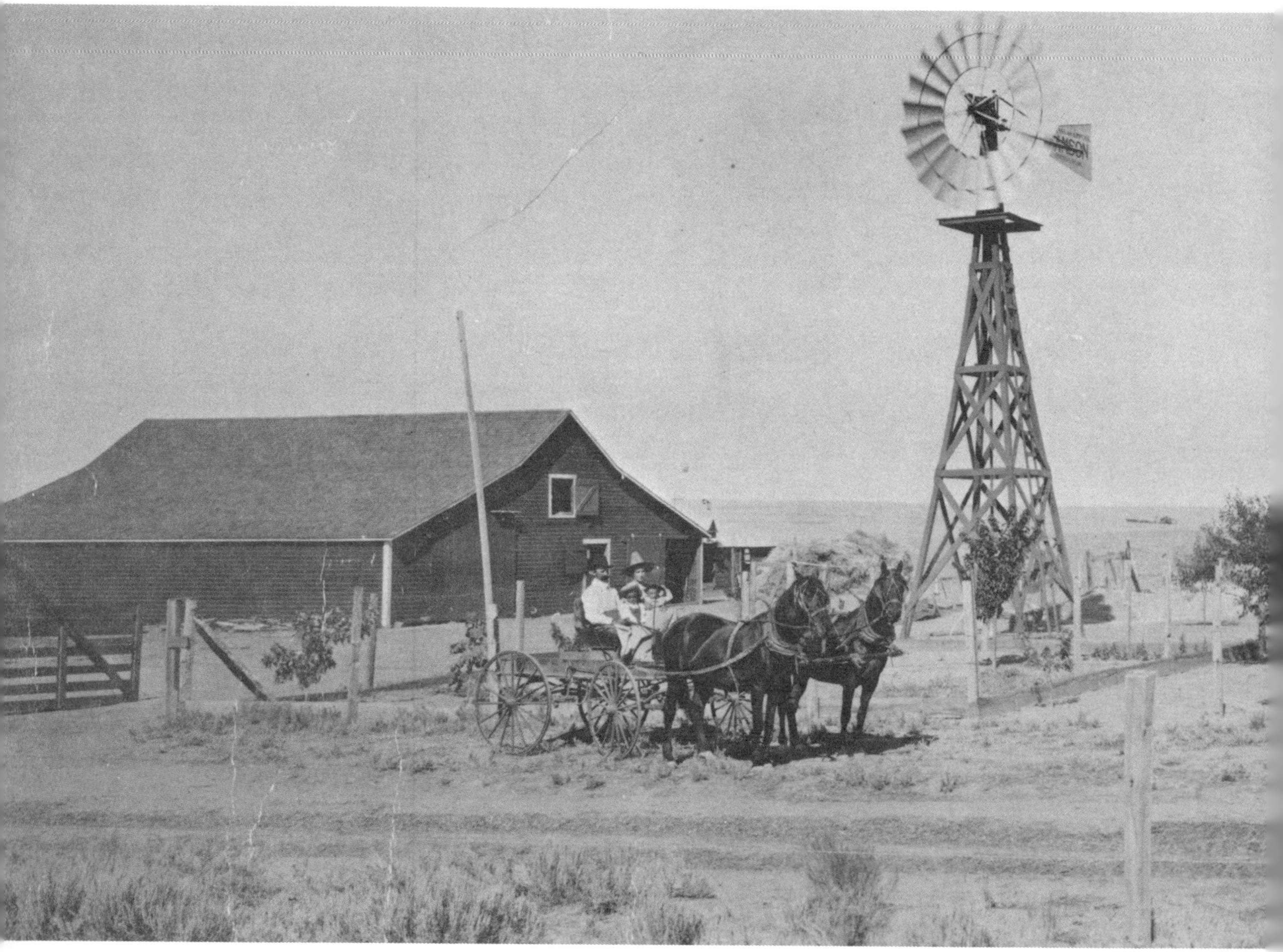

Fig. 53. Barn, house, and water supply of a central Washington wheat farm. This scene was typical of ranch life in the level areas of Washington. This was the farmstead of Jacob Reihs, Erby, Washington, August 5, 1908. Courtesy of Richard Walter.

Fig. 54. An all-black 6-in-hand team. Another Little International parade team at the University of Idaho, traveling in front of the Administration Building. Courtesy of Lester Kimberling

Fig. 55. A 3-bottom 12-inch mouldboard plow. This is a close-up of a 3-bottom gang plow commonly used in the soft white wheat area. Its trade name was "Flying Dutchman." The plow was pulled by eight horses hitched in tandem of fours. The right side (gee) horse of both the front and wheel teams walked in the plow furrow. This plow has three levers. One was used to shift the hitch to adjust the direction of the plow so it would cut a uniform furrow. Another adjusted the depth of furrow by raising or lowering the wheels. And the third rasied or lowered the upper (left) wheel to keep the plow level. Eight horses would plow an average of six acres per day. This plow is a museum item in Pioneer Village of Fort Walla Walla Park. Ross Watson Photo, 1971

Fig. 56. Disc cultivator, disc plow and sweep. The implements include a double disc, a single-disc plow and a sweep used to operate grain separators before the advent of the steam engine. These are museum items of the Lion's Club Museum, Cottonwood, Idaho. Joe Dvorak Photo, 1971

Fig. 57. Horses and plows — 1915. Six 8-horse plow teams are shown on a farm one and one-half miles northwest of Potlatch, Idaho, owned by Louie Gilmore. The total acreage plowed would average 45 acres per day. The 25-foot harrow was pulled by six horses and would cultivate an average of 30 acres per day. Courtesy of C. W. Ott

Fig. 58. Eighteen work mules. Mules owned by M. P. Bentley of Krupp, Washington, sired by "Taxpayer III." Their average weight ranged from 1,000 to 1,300 pounds with an average height-range of 13 to 14 hands. This was an ideal size for teams of six to 33 mules. These animals were photographed March 10, 1913. Courtesy of Richard Walter

Fig. 59. 8-mule plow team. Eight mules were hitched in tandem of two 4-mule teams to a 3-bottom gang plow. Butt-chain harnesses were used. This team was driven with four lines on the four outside mules. The gee mules of both teams walked in the furrow. Eveners were used to assign each mule the same pulling weight. This team would plow an average of seven acres per 10-hour day. Courtesy of Bill Walters

Fig. 60. A Horse-barn of the post World War I era. This was a typical barn built in 1920 for horses used in wheat production. It had all the conveniences for the efficient handling of four, six and eight horse teams. The barn was 80 feet long, 40 feet wide and 32 feet high. All hay and concentrate feeds were stored on the floor above the horse stalls. An 8-foot alley extended lengthwise down the barn between the mangers of the stalls. Twelve individual horse stalls were built on the south side (left), with six stalls for horses and four for cows on the north side. This barn was built by A. N. Keith. Joe Dvorak photo, 1972

Fig. 61. Round horse barn. This barn was built in 1917 by Thomas A. Leonard. The construction of the barn was engineered by the Potlatch Lumber Co., where the materials were purchased. This type of horse-barn construction was not a common one throughout the soft white wheat area. It is located on the old Moscow-Pullman highway. Phil Schofield photo

Fig. 62. A jackson fork at work. Hay was being moved to a hay mow or to a stack with a 4-tine Jackson fork.

Fig. 63. Hay harvesting with a buck-rake. This implement was called a "buck-rake." It was constructed with pointed poles 10 to 12 feet in length attached about 18 inches apart to a sturdy constructed frame. The poles were attached to the bottom of the frame in a manner that enabled them to slide over the surface of the ground. Two horses were hitched to a long double tree attached to the end of a beam. The beam extended from the rear of the frame to a distance of about 12 feet. The rake was pushed about the field to gather the windrowed hay and move it to a place of storage. At the stack, the hay was lifted into place with a crane.

Fig. 64. Stagecoaches, Culdesac, Idaho, 1900. These two stagecoaches, called mud-wagons, hauled passengers from Culdesac, Idaho, to Grangeville, Idaho, during the early 1900s. The stage on the left was of the same design as the old thorough-brace coach from Concord, New Hampshire. It was pulled by four horses, and carried eight or ten passengers. The thorough-braces were leather thongs that stretched from one axle to the other. On these the body of the coach swayed and rocked like a cradle. The coach on the right was constructed with springs between the body and the axles. The harnesses on stagecoach teams were fitted snug and tight. Harness of the wheel (rear) team was equipped with a breeching. A pole strap connected the breeching to the collar or neck-yoke. The lead team was hitched as close as possible to the wheel team. The distance was sufficient to keep the wheel team from stepping on the heels of the horses of the lead team. A team of four horses was driven with four lines. Robert Beale Photo

Fig. 65. Horsedrawn cabs in Moscow, Idaho. Neely's Cab Service used horses until 1919, when automobiles took over. The service had cars in 1908, but most people were afraid of them and always asked for horse cabs. Courtesy of Albert Neely

Fig. 66. First taxi service in Moscow, Idaho, circa, 1920. In 1919 horse-driven cabs were replaced by gas-powered cars with a top cruising rate of about 15 miles per hour. The "new" cabs included a 7-passenger Hudson, several 5-passenger Studebakers and a 7-passenger Franklin. Courtesy of Albert Neely

Fig. 67. Appaloosa buggy team, circa 1910. A team of Appaloosa horses were used by H. W. Goff, owner of an insurance agency in Colfax, Washington, to transport insurance salesmen through the wheat-growing areas. Courtesy of Abe McGregor Goff

Fig. 68. A 2-horse dirt mover. This scoop-type dirt mover was called a slip. It was used to move small quantities of dirt.

Fig. 69. Logging horses. Horses were the main source of power for moving logs in the woods from the beginning of logging to the early 1930s. Most logging teams consisted of only two horses. Four horses hitched in tandem of twos were used for an extremely large and heavy tree. Teams weighing not less than 1600 pounds per horse were the most desirable and most commonly used. Geldings with an even temperament seem to adapt more easily to this rugged work than mares. It was necessary that these horses could be trained within a short period of time. Many of the drivers did not use lines to control their teams, just voice commands. These horses were bred and grown on farms in the Soft White Wheat Area. They were too heavy for farm work but the right weight and size for logging purposes. One of the most common sources of these heavy horses was a ranch near Hay Station, Washington, owned by Phil Cox. This ranch had about 200 Percheron mares whose offspring were too heavy for use in wheat production. It was not uncommon to see a string of 4-year-old geldings weighing 1600 to 1800 pounds traveling on a road toward the timber areas of the mountains of Potlatch or Bovill, Idaho. I have seen as many as eight geldings in one string. The procedure was to lead one, with each of the other seven tied to his leader's tail. The man in charge would lead them with a saddle pony.

Fig. 70. A 4-horse fresno. The fresno was an implement designed to move dirt. It was used in building roads and irrigation ditches and in leveling areas where a building was to be constructed. Courtesy of Joe Dvorak

Fig. 71. Front view of two four-horse fresnos. Courtesy of Joe Dvorak

Fig. 72. Two 4-horse fresnos. Moving dirt with a fresno was rugged work for man and horse. Courtesy of Joe Dvorak

Fig. 73. Railroad construction with horses. Developing a road bed with horses and fresnos for the construction of the Spokane and Inland Empire Railroad, an electric-powered line, from Spokane, Washington, to Moscow, Idaho, 1908. Courtesy of C. W. Ott

Fig. 74. Horses and railroad building — 1908. Horse teams moved dirt to fill valleys, during the construction of the Spokane and Inland Empire Railroad in 1908. Courtesy of C. W. Ott

Fig. 75. A cutting horse at work. Courtesy of George B. Hatley

Part Three

THE COMBINE HARVESTER

"How are they able to harvest grain with combines on these steep hills?" The question has been asked many times by people who visit the soft white wheat area. Even after seeing a combine in operation on a hillside, some visitors remain incredulous. I remember clearly the amazed reactions of a group of people with whom I happened to be traveling one August day in 1929.

This was back in the days when you could see the scenic wonders of the West in a civilized way — by train. Instead of ignoring the landscape (as air travellers must) or degrading the environment (as motorists cannot escape doing), railroad passengers enjoyed the countryside and also did it no harm. I was on a Union Pacific train, in the vicinity of Starbuck, Washington — just north of Walla Walla. My fellow passengers in the observation car became fascinated with a spectacle that came into view on a steep hillside overlooking the track. A combine pulled by 33 horses had almost reached the top of the hill. As we looked up, the driver began making a 90-degree turn. With a big team, this was a complicated maneuver even on level land. Passengers near me were excited — and the excitement must have been felt elsewhere on the train. The engineer brought the train to a sudden halt and an enthralled audience of travellers watched intently as the driver skillfully executed the turn with the big team.

Skills of horsemanship enabled Pacific Northwest farmers to be pioneers in making efficient use of combines in the latter part of the 19th century. The first successful grain combine was built in Michigan, around 1836, but combine harvesting was not suited to the moist climate there at that time. Introduced into California in 1854, the combine gained considerable popularity on the large bonanza wheat farms. Several California firms were manufacturing combines in the 1880s — and these machines were purchased by Pacific Northwest wheat farmers. Later, inventors began developing machines especially suited to the conditions of the Pacific Northwest. Some of these machines were produced within the soft white wheat area.

Combine harvesting was a revolutionary concept which conservative farmers in many areas declined to accept. Stewart H. Holbrook, in *Machines of Plenty,* says it was natural "that pure mythology should play a part in delaying the advent of the new machine." He notes that constant repetition in farming circles kept in circulation the myth "that combines left a good third or half of the crop on the ground. Apparently, no one took the trouble to measure the waste, if waste there was."

While farmers in other regions maintained their cautious "wait-and-see" attitude regarding the combine, farmers of the soft white wheat area were buying the new harvesters in large numbers. These combines were large and heavy, requiring the use of big teams. And the big teams had to be hitched together efficiently in order that each horse might handle its fair share of the load. A 32-horse team will not provide eight times the power of a 4-horse team if only a portion of the horses in the big team are working as they should. Equalization of the load was the goal of inventors who designed big-team hitches. The most satisfactory hitch for combining and other big-team operations was invented by Peter Schandoney of Sacramento, California.

The Schandoney Equalizing Hitch, patented in 1892, became popular throughout the Pacific Northwest. Because one essential feature of Schandoney's invention was a three-looped piece of metal called the cloverleaf, the Schandoney hitch was commonly known as the "cloverleaf hitch".

The idea for the equalizing hitch came to Peter Schandoney when he was a youth working on the family farm in the Sacramento Valley. While driving a 10-mule string plow team, he observed that the more energetic mules pulled most of the load because the lazy animals could pace themselves in order to avoid much pulling. The hitch then in use was called the "dead hitch". It was constructed by attaching five two-horse double trees of the stretcher type on a log chain for hitching 10 horses in tandem of twos. The Schan-

Fig. 76. 32-horse team, 1900. This 20-foot ground-powered combine was owned by Charles Arthur Snow and Ed Snow near Moscow, Idaho. Leather-tugged harnesses were used on the wheel (or rear) team and the next three 6-horse teams. Butt chains were used on the 2-horse lead team and the following six horses. This was about the time of the introduction of butt chains. Butt-chain harnesses were more convenient for big teams because they required less time to hitch and unhitch. This combine team of 32 horses was driven with two lines. Mothers of colts were always hitched on the side of the combine opposite the reel and sickle. If the mothers were hitched on the reel and sickle side, the colts would be in the uncut grain and would interfere with the operation of the sickle and reel. The crew was composed of a driver, mechanic, headerman, sack sewer and sack jig. The sack jig filled the sacks. The mechanic was the boss of the operation. This machine was cutting an oat crop in a rich lowland area. The harvesting of oats increased the work of the sack sewer and sack jig. Oats have more bulk per unit of weight than wheat and the sacks are filled faster. Courtesy of the Library of the University of Idaho.

Fig. 77. Five 33-horse combine teams. These five "Oregon Specialists" were built by Hold Manufacturing Company of Stockton, California, in 1904. They were owned by the Drumheller brothers whose ranch was located on Dry Gulch Creek in Walla Walla County, Washington. A total of seven combines were in the shipment to Walla Walla; one was purchased by Henry Ringer and one by Henry Penner. They were ground-powered and were pulled by horses and mules. This photo became famous. According to Stewart H. Holbrook in *Machines of Plenty:* "Here was a picture fit to astound almost anybody, and it went as promptly as possible into the souvenir postcard trade. For many years a favorite scene showed 165 head of horses pulling monstrous combines across an ocean of wheat." Courtesy of Robert Beale Pomeroy, Washington

Fig. 78. 32-horse team, 1911. This is a 32-horse team of Cleveland Bays and Hambletonians. The team, hitched in tandem of five sixes and two leaders, is pulling a ground-powered combine owned by the Ferguson brothers in 1911. The Cleveland Bays were from a group of three carloads purchased in Ohio in 1909 by Myron Ferguson, who was a horse dealer. At one time he had 2,000 horses on the ranch. Cleveland Bays and Hambletonians matured at a weight range of 1,350 to 1,500 pounds. These weights were ideal for big teams on the steep Palouse hills. Soon after 1912, the Fergusons purchased a large steam engine to pull the combine. Conversion of the combine to steam power was the work of Archie Ferguson (oldest son of Myron). This conversion proved to be unsatisfactory for the pulling on the Palouse Hills and the combine was converted back to horse power the following year. Courtesy of Dave Ferguson

doney hitch distributed the load among the horses or mules. As employed on combines, the hitch required one cloverleaf for each 6-horse team. The equalizing effect of this arrangement can be observed in the diagram I present in this section. Certainly, the driver of the combine could see which horses and which 6-horse units were not performing their assigned duties.

An invention of seemingly modest magnitude, the Schandoney hitch was in fact a major advance for Pacific Northwest agriculture. Large-scale wheat farmers of the region benefitted also as engines were developed to supplement the power of horses in agriculture. The nation's first gas-powered combines appeared in the state of Washington several years before World War I. Before the turn of the century, steam-powered combines were available from California manufacturers but this use of the steam engine was not very practical in the soft white wheat area. Despite the mechanical problems encountered with the gas engines, they were convenient, requiring fewer workers and horses. When the power to operate the combine was shifted from the ground (or bull wheel) to a small gas engine (usually a two-cycle model), the number of horses was reduced from 33 to 27 and the number of men from six to five for a 20-foot sickle combine.

In the chronology of agricultural development, Pacific Northwest farmers were beginning to shift to combine harvesting at about the same time that farmers in the Midwest were adopting the twine binder. The goal of Pacific Northwest wheat producers was large-scale production, using the most efficient harvesting methods possible. They found horse-propelled combines well suited for their purpose.

Comparative costs of combining and traditional harvesting were studied in 1919 from several different views. One set of statistics showed combines had harvested wheat at 4.3 cents per bushel, while the cost of harvesting with binder and thresher approached 20 cents a bushel. Another report showed that the cost of harvesting an acre of grain by combine would range from $1 to $1.50 per acre, as compared to a cost from $3.36 to $4.22 per acre by other methods.

COMBINE HARVESTER TEAMS

The number of horses used to pull a combine-harvester varied with the length of sickle-bar, the contour of the area, and whether the combine

Fig. 79. 24-horse combine-harvester team. This harvesting operation must have required the driver to make short, sharp turns since four instead of six horses were used on the wheel (or tongue) team. These were hitched in positions nearest to the tongue. Four men were used to operate the team and machinery — the driver, header man, machinist and sack-sewer. The crop on this field was too light for the needs of the sack-jig. This team, owned and operated by Conrad Walter of Odessa, Washington, was photographed in July 1910. Courtesy of Richard Walter

71

Fig. 80. 20-horse combine-harvester team. In the plateau areas of central Washington, fewer horses or mules were required to pull harvesting equipment than in the areas of steep slopes in Whitman or Walla Walla counties. The fields were generally rectangular in shape, enclosing 320 or 640 acres, and a team would travel half a mile or more before making a turn. The acre yields of grain and straw were lower in the plateau areas. Twenty horses could pull a 20-foot, ground-powered combine here while 33 would be needed on the steep slopes. The 2-horse team with a small wagon was used to haul the scattered sacks to an area where they could be loaded on regular wagons for delivery to wheat stations. The combine crew of four included a driver, mechanic, header man and sack-sewer. Fritz Kisler was the owner and operator of this ground-powered combine-harvester in August 1909. Courtesy of Richard Walter

Fig. 81. 24-horse-and-mule combine-harvester team. Six mules and 18 horses were used to pull this combine. Undoubtedly, the owner did not have enough horses or mules for a complete team of either. Since mules travel slower uphill and faster downhill than horses, it was a logical procedure to distribute them throughout the hitch. There are six positions in which an animal must work next to the chain and, since mules are not easily disturbed by the lead chains, one was assigned to each position. Four animals were used on the wheel (or rear) team to avoid interference with the reel and sickle during the turning operation. This was a ground-powered combine-harvester owned by G. Graedel, Irby, Washington, August, 1912. Courtesy of Richard Walter

75

Fig. 82. 26-mule combine-harvester team. Two lines from the two lead mules controlled the 26-mule team. Filled wheat sacks were being loaded on two wagons (connected in tandem) and hauled with a 6-horse team. A 6-horse team could conveniently haul 60 sacks of wheat, 90 sacks of barley or 100 sacks of oats if the soil was compact and there were no steep slopes. This ground-powered combine-harvester was owned by M. P. Bentley of Irby, Washington, August 1914. Courtesy of Richard Walter

Fig. 83. 26-horse combine-harvester team. Four 6-horse teams hitched in tandem and controlled with two lines on a 2-horse team were used to pull a 20-foot sickle-bar combine. As the machine cut the crop, the straw was placed in the windrows and wheat-filled sacks were dropped in the same area. J. W. Baird of Lamona, Washington, owned and operated this ground-powered combine-harvester during August of 1914. Courtesy of Richard Walter

Fig. 84. Combine-harvesters using 31 and 24 horses. These two ground-powered combine-harvesters were owned and operated by L. F. Bentley and M. Bentley of Odessa, Washington. Each team used four horses on the wheel (rear) team for short-turning purposes. Three horses were used to lead the 31-horse team and two horses were used to lead the 24-horse team and each team was driven with two lines. The jerk-line was used for driving the 8-horse team which pulled three wagons (coupled in tandem) for hauling wheat to the railroad warehouse. The jerk-line was fastened to the bridle-bit of the gee-horse of the rear teams. A wooden stick was used to control the haw-horse of the lead team. A 2-horse team and wagon was used to collect the scattered, wheat-filled sacks for loading the three wagons of the 8-horse team. Sixty-five horses were used in this operation to harvest an average of approximately 60 acres per day. Courtesy of Richard Walter

81

Fig. 85. 27-horse team, 1926. Twenty-seven horses hitched in tandem of four sixes and three leaders are pulling a gas-engine combine in the Palouse hills near Moscow, Idaho. Even though the combine operated with an engine, horses were still needed to pull it over the steep hills. Hodgins Drug Photo

Fig. 86. Two 27-horse combine teams. These ground-powered combines are harvesting a crop on the Charles Hofer place near Pullman, Washington. Six horses were used on the rear team, which indicates that there were no problems in turning the combine and no steep-sloped ravines. A canopy protected the sack sewers from the sun. A man on a saddle pony ran errands, such as going to headquarters for repairs or disentangling horses and harnesses in case of mix-ups. This picture shows the method of dumping the sacked grain and straw. Bill Wallers Photo

Fig. 87. 33-mule combine. Thirty-three mules pulled this gas-engine operated combine owned and operated by Carl Penner, Walla Walla, Washington. The mules were sometimes driven with four lines — two from the three leaders and two from the 6-horse team just to the rear of the leaders. With this system, nine mules turned the combine team. The 6-horse team was directed to begin the turn a few seconds before the lead team. The extra horse was used as a saddle horse for doing errands, such as getting repair parts. Courtesy of Carl Penner

machinery was operated with ground-power or an auxiliary engine. The common-sized team for a ground-powered combine with a 16-foot sickle-bar was 33 horses. Most of the combine operators had five teams of six-abreast and three leaders. A 44-horse team had five teams of eight-abreast and four leaders.

The first ground-powered combine used the "dead hitch." Each pair of horses pulled direct from the combine. Horses used with this hitch were subjected to considerable torture, since it was difficult for the driver to regulate the load for each animal.

Eventually, several hitches were designed to assign each horse his share of the load. Among these were the Talkenton, Harrington, Pendleton, and "the Schandoney equalizing hitch." The Schandoney (sometimes referred to as the cloverleaf) was eventually used by almost all combine operators. The Schandoney hitch was constructed on the leverage principle so that it is a perfect equalizer for any number of animals. It was especially useful for combine harvesters, where 14 to 44 animals were required. Instead of the three chains used in the dead hitch, the Schandoney used only one — and this eliminated unnecessary crowding and skinning or bruising of the animals' legs.

There were many problems for the driver in areas of steep slopes with deep gulches running at right angles to the main ridge. In crossing these gulches, the lead team would be on top of a ridge with the center of the hitch above the backs of the center teams and the combine on a ridge to the rear. Wide belly bands, securely fastened to the tugs of the harness, prevented the collars from choking the horses of the center teams.

Some operators used only four horses in the (rear) tongue team, with the two center positions next to the tongue vacant. This prevented interference of the driver's seat with the tongue team when the combine was moving down the steep slope of the gulch, while the team was moving up the next slope. Also, in level areas where the field was large and turns were few and far between, many operators used only four horses on the tongue with the outside positions vacant. Sharp turns crowded the right outside horse into the reel and sickle when all six were used.

The Schandoney hitch presented a problem when climbing a steep slope. Horses or mules soon learned that by rushing forward and remaining ahead of their co-workers they could reduce their own load. This problem could be solved by an alert driver who would regulate the assignments by slowing the rate of travel of the entire team. The problem could also be corrected through the use of buckstraps.

The first day of harvesting with a combine team was generally exciting. If the team consisted of horses that had been rested and well-fed for a period of 30 days or more, the horses were apt to buck or balk. Some would be stepping in the lead hitches and stepping across lead chains. Mules or horses that had been over-worked and under-nourished seldom became excited.

Fig. 88. 27-horse combine-harvester team. Two lines on a 3-horse lead-team was used to control this combine team. The use of a jerk-line on a 6-horse team hitched to two wagons (in tandem) is clearly shown. Straw was being collected with a 2-horse hay wagon. This outfit was owned and operated by L.F. Bentley of Odessa, Washington. Courtesy of Richard Walter

Fig. 89. The first of three views of a holt combine near Moscow, Idaho during the 1920s. The 14-foot sickle bar combine requires 14 horses and four men for its operation.

The duties of the men are: a teamster, header man, sack sewer and machine mechanic. The machinery is operated with an auxiliary engine. Hodgins Drug Store Photos

Fig. 90. The second of three views of the holt combine. The straw and filled sacks of wheat are collected and dumped at regular intervals. The filled sacks are dumped in windrows of six at one time.

Most drivers of combine teams had a set of bells on the lead team. These bells were placed on the hames of the horses with the lines. The bells were generally fastened to the top of the hames and as the animals moved the bells would toll in cadence. This would contribute to a uniform rate of travel.

Because bells were attached to the animals with the lines, the driver had a convenient method of starting a team. As soon as the driver pulled on the lines, the leaders would move, causing the bells to jingle. This alerted the entire team that it was time to move.

COMBINE CREW

The number of men required to operate a pull-type combine varied from four to six, plus one man at headquarters. Size of team, length of sickle bar, and bushel yield per acre determined the manpower needs. Horses used in pulling the combine ranged from 18 to 44. Numbers of horses per team were of the order 18, 21, 33 and 44. Eighteen-horse teams were hitched in tandem of three fours and two leaders. The 21 and27 and 33-horse teams were hitched in tandems of sixes with three leaders. a 44-horse team was hitched in tandem of eights with four leaders. Ground-powered combines required more horses than combines with engines used to operate the machinery. Sixteen and 20-foot combines used more horses than shorter lengths.

Teams of 33 and 44 horses required an extra man called the "roustabout." He rode a saddle horse along the left side of the team. He was available for handling problems that developed within the team. Since cars of that era did not operate easily in stubble fields, the roustabout rode his horse on many necessary errands.

Length of sickle bar and yield of wheat determined the number of men needed for sacking the grain. A yield of 25 to 40 bushels per acre with a 20-foot sickle bar required two men for sacking the grain. One man filled the sacks. He was called the "sack jig." The second man sewed the sacks and dropped them down the chute. The chute held six sacks. When filled the sacks were released.

The header man had the duty of adjusting the height of the sickle bar for minimum straw length. The mechanic kept the machinery in working order. The man at headquarters fed the horses, checked water supply, mended harness, and purchased supplies as needed.

Combine driver, header man, sack jig, sack sewer, and roustabout hitched, unhitched, watered, curried, and harnessed the horses. With a team of 33 horses, the combine driver had nine, header man six, sack jig six, sack sewer six and roustabout six. It required 10 seconds for the crew to unhitch a combine team. A total of 10 minutes would find a team unhitched, watered, and eating at the manger. Time required to hitch a team to combine was greater than time required for unhitching. Men and horses were more sluggish and tended to move at a slower rate, especially after the noon meal. Time required to feed, curry, and harness a horse in the morning would average about six minutes. Time required to remove harness from a horse in the evening averaged about 20 seconds.

THE JERK-LINE

When a single line is used to drive a team, it is called the "jerk-line". A jerk-line team may include two, four, six or eight horses or mules hitched in tandem of twos or a combine team of 18, 22, 33 or 46 hitched in tandem of sixes or eights. The jerk-line was not used on the steep hills along the Palouse River in Whitman County, Washington, or in other areas of steep slopes. However, it was a common method used to drive big teams in the level areas of central Washington.

The procedure used to drive a team with the jerk-line varied with the individual driver and the temperament of the horse or mule assigned to the position. The operation was naturally more successful with a horse or mule and driver who had worked together over a period of years, especially when the driver had trained the mule or horse. Any animal selected for the jerk-line position was one that was strong, alert, and of an even temperament.

The horse or mule was fitted with a bridle that was strong and snug. Some teamsters used a bridle without blinds.

The jerk-line was passed through the rings on the hames of the horses directly in the rear of the jerk-line animal. The line passed through the left hame ring of the jerk-line animal and on through the left ring of the bridle bit. The end of the line was then snapped to a ring of the bridle located above and just to the rear of the left eye. A snaffle bit was generally used. However, after a horse or mule had worked in this position for years, an ordinary bridle with the jerk-line snapped to the bit ring was adequate for controlling the team.

Fig. 91. Rear view of the holt combine. The rear view shows the header man, mechanic with the leveling device and the sack sewer in their respective positions.

Fig. 92. 40-horse combine-harvester team. This is a ground-powered 20-foot sickle bar Holt combine, pulled with 40 horses. The team was hitched in tandem of six 6-horse teams with a 4-horse lead team. Courtesy of Clifford W. Ott

If the driver desired to turn the entire team to the right, he gave a series of short jerks, which caused the jerk-line animal to lift his head and step sidewise to the right. The entire team of 4 to 33 or more animals was under the control of the jerk-line animal. The other animals of the lead team were controlled by jockey sticks and check straps. When the jerk-line animal stepped to the right or gee direction, he automatically forced the remainder of the lead team to the right.

If the driver desired to turn the entire team left (or haw direction), he exerted a gentle consistent pull on the jerk-line. The jerk-line animal stepped sidewise to the left, moving the entire team in that direction.

THE SCHANDONEY HITCH

This method of hitching horses or mules to a 33-horse combine employed several principles of equalizing the load. The cloverleaf was a necessary part of every 6-horse hitch. The ends of 3-horse eveners were fastened to each side of the cloverleaf.

The second six were assigned a slightly lighter load than the first six, with each succeeding team having a lighter load than the preceding one.

The three lead horses were not assigned any part of the combine load. All of their efforts went to leading and guiding the other 30 horses.

The key to the success of this hitch was the cloverleaf. It gave flexibility and contributed to

an easy system of distributing the load among the horses.

The team was controlled with two lines on the leaders. The lines were placed on the two outside horses, with checks to the bridle rings of the center horse.

The remaining 30 horses were kept in position with buckstraps, checks, and sticks. The buckstraps of the outside horses were fastened to a single tree of the inside horse, while the buckstraps of the inside horses were fastened to the lead chains. If the leaders slowed, the lead chains slowed the inside horses, which in turn slowed the outside horses of each 6-horse team.

Jockey sticks were fastened between the hames of the inside horse and the chinstraps of the outside horse to prevent crowding. Check straps were fastened between the bits of each horse and to the lead chain.

After a combine team had worked together for 10 days or more, the jockey sticks and buck straps could be removed since each horse had them learned his place and duties.

In areas of steep slopes, two lines were used to drive the entire team. Some drivers used four lines — two for the lead team plus two lines on the six horses to the rear of the lead team. This enabled the driver to begin turning the first six-abreast before the lead team. This reduced the load on the lead team and contributed to a faster and easier turn.

Fig. 93. Schandoney combine hitch for a 33-horse team. Courtesy of Robert Beale

Fig. 94. Location of the cloverleaf in the Schandoney hitch. This photo shows the location of the cloverleaf in relation to the lead chain triple trees and singletrees. Each and every horse was assigned a definite share of the land. The Schandoney hitch was sometimes called the "cloverleaf hitch." This photo was taken in Pioneer Village, Fort Walla Walla Museum complex. Ross Watson Photo, 1971

Fig. 95. The cloverleaf. Twelve inches was the maximum width and maximum length of the cloverleaf. It was attached with clevises at the center ends of the 3-horse triple trees.

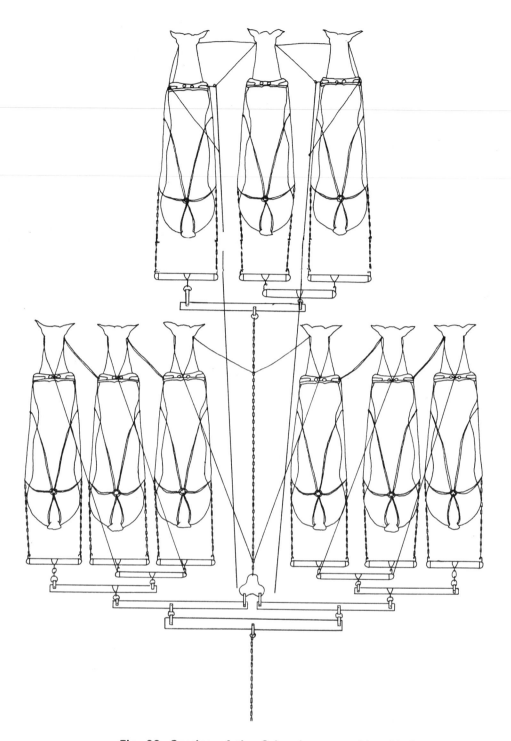

Fig. 96. Section of the Schandoney combine hitch.
Nine horses of a 33-horse Schandoney combine-hitch are
presented to show the method of hitching and controlling
the team. The diagram shows the locations of the
buckstraps, jockey sticks and check straps.

Fig. 97. Front view of a combine harvester. This shows the driver's seat at the top of a ladder that extends over the first team. The sickle and reel are in view on the left. The header man's leveling control was to the rear of the driver's seat — the wheel with extended spokes. The bull wheel is shown on the right side of the machine. The carrier for filled sacks is located just above the bull wheel. The sack sewer's seat is located at the top of the ladder. This exhibit is in the Fort Walla Walla Pioneer Village. Ross Watson Photo, 1971

Fig. 98. Steam-powered combine. Soon after 1912, the Ferguson family of the Rim Rock Ranch five miles southwest of Colton purchased a large engine to pull their combine. The combine was rebuilt to include a 28-foot sickle with two 14-foot reels. The steam engine furnished all power, which included pulling the combine and operating the separator and the header. The conversion was unsatisfactory for pulling on steep Palouse hills and, since the steam engine was a potential fire hazard, the combine was converted back to horse power the following year. Courtesy of Dave Ferguson

Fig. 99. Converted self-propelled Holt combine, 1919. A horse-drawn ground-powered combine was converted to a self-propelled machine by John Wells in 1919 near Asotin, Washington. An internal combustion engine was built into the front part of the machine to pull and operate the header and separator. The machine was moved to the Uniontown, Washington, area but was not adapted to the hills. It was eventually converted to a stationary thresher. The converted horse-drawn machines were generally too cumbersome to operate with any degree of efficiency. Courtesy of Clifford W. Ott

Fig. 100. An Allis Chalmers combine. This combine was harvesting wheat near Moscow, Idaho. Its construction was similar to the Idaho National Harvester, except it was pulled with a tractor and the sickle-bar was on the left side of the separator. Courtesy of J. W. Martin

Fig. 101. View of the right side of the 6-foot pull-combine. Courtesy of J. W. Martin

Fig. 102. Rhodes combine harvester, 1915. The Rhodes Combine Harvester was first built in 1912 on the south east corner of Main and Eighth in Moscow, Idaho. The plant was eventually moved to Dishman, Washington, near Spokane. This machine was a light-weight, all-steel combine designed specifically for efficient harvesting of wheat grown on the steep hills of the area encompassing Latah County, Idaho and Whitman County, Washington. The men involved in the company included:

Directors:
J. J. Miller
C. L. MacKenzie
Otto Glasser, jeweler, Colfax, Wash.
W. M. Rhodes
Chas. Dezell

Officers:
J. J. Miller, President, Colfax, Wash.
C. L. Mackenzie, Vice-President, banker, Colfax, Wash.
Chas. Dezell, Secretary, hardware, Lacrosse, Wash.
W. A. Mackenzie, Treasurer, banker, Colfax, Wash.
F. S. Ratliff, Supt. Construction, Moscow, Ida.

Fig. 103. Front and rear view of the Rhodes combine harvester. An advertisement listed these specifications:

All Steel Cylinder
Separator
Waukesha Motor
Main Wheels Diameter
Horses required
Magneto
Men required
Capacity
Leveling capacity
Hyatt Roller Bearings
With or without Straw Dump
Weight, approximately 9000 pounds
24 inches
34 inches
50 H.P.
54 in. 12 in.
16 to 20
Eisemann
Four
25 to 35 acres per day
40 inches

Courtesy of Lila Hawley

Fig. 104. Rhodes combine near Colfax, Washington. A Rhodes Combine Harvester owned and operated by M. Kroll near Colfax, Washington. It is being pulled with 16 horses hitched in tandem of fours. Courtesy of Lila Hawley, Moscow, Idaho

Fig. 105. Rhodes combine near Wilcox, Washington. A Rhodes Combine Harvester owned and operated by Gus Heilsburg, near Wilcox, Washington. Twenty-two horses were hitched in tandem of three-sixes and a four-horse lead team. Courtesy of Lila Hawley, Moscow, Idaho

Fig. 106. A horse-operated thresher. Thirteen horses supplied power for operating this separator. This separator used 13 horses — six poles with two horses each and one with three horses. Two different outfits are shown in this picture. A heading outfit was cutting and stacking grain, while a horse-operated separator is threshing the stacked grain. A Jackson fork was pulling the headings from the stack to the derrick table. The separator was called a "halfmoon" because of the method of stacking the straw. The straw was carried from the separator with an elevator by an endless draper. The top of the elevator could be moved to and fro. This produced a stack of straw resembling a halfmoon. This was the method commonly used before the development of the "wind blower."

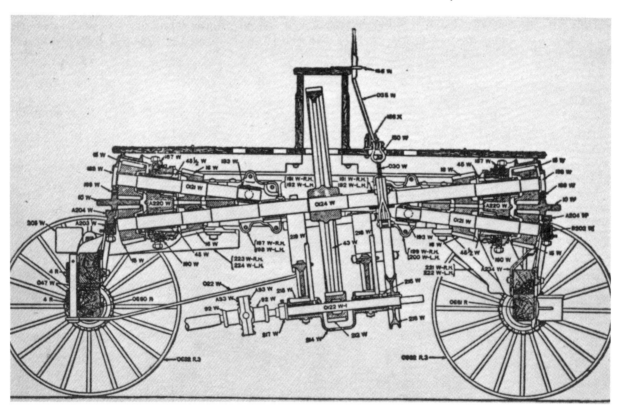

Fig. 107. Detail view of an iron frame horse-power. Courtesy of J. I. Case

Part Four
THE STATIONARY
THRESHER

The term "Stationary Thresher" refers to a method of separating the grain from the straw and chaff while the mechanical equipment is located in a convenient place of the area to be harvested. The headings and bundles may be stacked previous to the time of threshing or they may be hauled and threshed simultaneously.

The first separator was a small fanning mill powered with a horse on a treadmill. This method was followed by the "half moon" separator and was powered with horses hitched to a "sweep," often referred to as the merry-go-round.

During the period from 1900 to the 1920s, the steam engine was developed to power the separator along with the wind blower to remove the straw from the separator. The partnership of the multiple-hitch horse teams along with the use of the steam engine for powering the separator increased the efficiency of producing wheat during the years of 1916 to 1918. This increase in the total production of wheat throughout the Pacific Northwest was a contributing factor in the winning of World War I by the Allies.

Furthermore, the horse and steam engine combination also contributed to the first national surplus of wheat in 1919 which continued throughout the 1920s. This situation reduced the price of wheat to the extent that it was necessary for Congress to offer the wheat farmer some method of relief which resulted in the introduction of the McNary-Haugen bill.

During the period between 1910 and the 1920s, the steam engine was gradually replaced by the internal combustion engine. The internal combustion engine had the advantage of being able to pull heavier loads at a faster rate than the steam engine. It was also more convenient for belt power since it did not require equipment to supply fuel in the form of wood or straw and to supply large quantities of water.

THE HORSE-POWER

The horse-power was the principal means of operating threshing machines before the steam engine. A horse-power (or merry-go-round) was a simple mechanism constructed to transfer power from horses to a threshing-machine. Horses were hitched to ends of sweeps and traveled in a circle.

The number of horses used varied with the work load. When desired for light work, the regular 12-horse-power with six sweeps could be used with only six horses by tying up equalizers on the empty sweeps and attaching teams to alternate sweeps, or by hitching a single horse to each sweep.

The sweeps of the 12-horse-power and smaller sizes were 12 feet seven inches long and their ends moved in a circle, the circumference of which was 79 feet.

The sweeps of the 14-horse-power were 14 feet long and their ends moved in a circle, the circumference of which was 89 feet. Horses would ordinarily travel around the 79-foot circle two and one-half times a minute, and around the 89-foot circle two and one-fourth times a minute, in either case covering about two and one-fourth miles per hour.

SACK SEWERS

Before the development of grain elevators, wheat was sacked at the time of harvest, regardless of the type of harvesting equipment used. Only one sack sewer was needed for a combine with a 16-foot sickle and acre yields of 25 bushels or less. A sack sewer and sack jig were required with 20-foot combines cutting wheat that yielded more than 25 bushels.

Stationary threshers with separator-cylinders of 32 to 48 inches would require a jig and two sewers. Two sack sewers and a jig could fill and pile an average of 2,200 sacks, or approximately 5,000 bushels, in 15 hours. This credits each sack sewer for sewing, carrying, and piling 1,100 sacks per day — or one and two-tenths sack per minute.

The sacking mechanism was constructed with an elevator that carried the kernels from an auger at the bottom of the separator to a point about

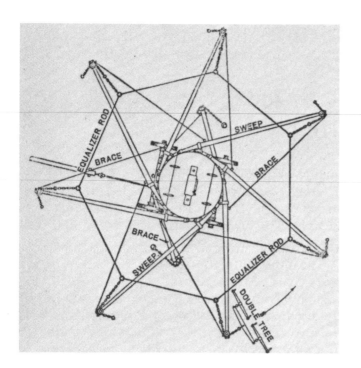

Fig. 108. Top view of power with sweeps attached. The diagram shows the top view of a 14-horse-power with "sweeps" braces, and equalizer-rods attached. The sweeps were attached to the bull-wheel which revolved when in operation. The sweeps were kept in position with braces while the equalizers assigned an equal load to each team. The driver stood in the center, atop the bull-wheel attachment. He had at his convenience a brake which could be controlled by hand or foot. The direction of gearing could be reversed when reverse motion was necessary for driving machinery other than Case separators. This process included the turning over of the bull-wheel, the interchanging of the short shafts and the reversing of the spur wheel shaft. The direction in which the tumbling-rods revolved was reversed so they would turn in the same direction as that in which the horses walked. Courtesy of J. I. Case Co.

Fig. 109. Threshing near Steptoe, Washington in 1893. This is the threshing operation of Ed Davis, son of Cash-up Davis, who built and owned the hotel atop Steptoe Butte. The operation includes a 14-foot sickle-bar header, four header-boxes and a grain separator powered by horses. The horse-power shown on the left consists of six sweeps with two horses on each sweep. Three horses are used to pull each header-box. Eight horses are hitched to the header. A total of 32 horses are used in the operation. The work assignments include: one man to drive the horses powering the sweeps, one mechanic for the separator, four box-team drivers, one sack-sewer, one man for stacking straw, one spiker-pitcher for assisting box-drivers in unloading, one header-box loader and a driver of the header (header puncher). The header cuts an average of 18 acres per day with an average acre yield of 30 bushels. This represented a daily production of approximately 450 sacks of wheat. The pay scale for the crew for a 12-hour day was as follows:

Header-box drivers	$1.25 per day	Header puncher	$5.00 per day
Header-box loader	$2.50 per day	Separator-mechanic	$6.00 per day
Spike-pitcher	$2.50 per day	Sweep-driver	$4.00 per day
Sack-sewer	$3.50 per day	Horses	$0.25 per day
Straw-stacker	$1.25 per day		

The market value of the wheat was 18 cents per bushel.

seven feet above the top of the separator where it was emptied into an 8-inch tube. This tube was about 20 feet long. The end of the tube had a V-shaped attachment with two spouts. A burlap bag was attached to the end of each spout. The bottom of the bag was placed crosswise of a 4"x-4"x6' piece of wood to force the grain in the corners of the bag.

After each sack was filled, it was set between the legs of one of the sewers. Two full sacks of wheat, one on top of the other, were used as a seat by the sack sewer. If the sewer was right-handed, the sack was placed with one side near the right knee and the other next to the upper part of the left leg.

The needle had a broad blade with sharp edges and a spring clip on one side of the needle eye. This enabled the sewer to thread the needle with a simple flip.

The sewer placed the right flap of the sack under the left, forming an ear at each side. Quickly, the sewer flipped a double half-hitch around the right ear of the bag. He next sent the needle back and forth through the top for nine to 12 stitches and two more half-hitches to form the second ear. A sewer who made only nine stitches in a 140-pound sack of wheat was a very poor craftsman. A sack with only nine stitches could have leaks at both sides of the seam.

When he was finished sewing, the sewer placed the sack on his left, picked it up in his arms and carried it about 10 yards to a pile.

A majority of sewers were longshoremen who spent the summers in the harvest fields.

BOAT TRANSPORTATION, PRE-RAILROAD

River transportation got its start as early as 1851 when the Bradfort Brothers and J. Van Gregen began a boating business at The Dalles on the Columbia River.[2] They built one of the first steam boats in the Pacific Northwest. In 1860, the Oregon Steam Navigation Company was formed with Captain J. C. Ainsworth as head. In 1861, their steamer, "The Colonel Wright" sailed as far as Lewiston, Idaho.

Freight of these boats included cattle, horses, farm machinery, wheat, gold, ore, and passengers plus mail.

Snake River boats were the major transportation carriers for supplies and shipments of farm and mining products until the railroads reached the area. The over-all transportation system of the soft white wheat area was improved in 1873, when a "narrow gauge" railroad was completed to connect Walla Walla, Washington, with steamboat landings at Wallula. It was not until November 10, 1883, that the "iron horses" steamed into Colfax, Washington. After the railroads became established, the river boat business tended to dwindle.

WAGON TEAMS

Four-horse teams usually hauled harvested wheat to railroad stations. If the ranch was more than six miles from the railroad station, eight horses or mules in one team hauled wagons hitched in tandem. Six horses were hitched with four in the rear and two in the lead, or in tandem of twos. Eight horses were hitched in tandem of fours. Occasionally, eight horses or mules were hitched in tandem of twos.

In level areas of central Washington the jerk line was used. In areas where roads had curves and hills to climb, eight lines were used on eight horses hitched in tandem of twos.

GLOSSARY OF WAGON TERMS

Axle-tree — a non-revolving shaft that connects opposite wheels of a wagon in front and in rear.

Bolster — a 5"x5" piece of hard lumber with uprights at each end, sitting on the axle trees under the wagon bed. The rear bolster was fastened solid to the rear axle. The front bolster allowed rotation of the front axle.

Coupling — a U-shaped structure attached to the rear-axle that connected the rear-axle with the reach.

Coupling-pin — a long bolt used to connect the reach to the coupling.

Fifth-wheel — the semi-revolving mechanism of the front axle. The front-bolster, with an attached steel plate, sat on a steel plate attached to the front-axle. The kingpin passed through a hole in the bolster, steel plates, front axle and reach. This mechanism enabled the front wheels to change directions.

Kingpin — a large, long, iron pin that connects the reach, bolster, and front-axle.

Reach — a pole or a 2"x6" piece of lumber that connects the rear-axle to the front-axle.

Standards — the uprights at the end of the bolsters. These hold the wagon bed in position.

Fig. 110. A donkey engine. The picture shows one of the early uses of steam to replace horse-drawn "sweeps" in threshing. This engine is a modification of the wood-burning donkey engine, the type of steam engine used in the woods to move logs. The engine shown in the picture was built on wheels and moved by horses. The donkey engine used in the woods was built on skids and moved from place to place with a cable and windlass. In both engines, the smoke stack was directly over the fire box. The separator was the same construction as that used with the sweep. A carrier moved the straw from the separator and men moved the straw from the end of the carrier. Many of the straw stacks had the appearance of a half-moon; this was the origin of the name "half-moon separator". The tripod-shaped gadget between the engine and separator was part of the derrick table, which was set between the ends of the wheat stacks. One end of the feeder was placed on the table to carry the headings to the separator. A loaded Jackson fork which used two horses to drag the headings from the stack to the derrick table is hanging between the poles of the tripod. The horses were hitched to a cable that passed through a pulley attached to the table and went to a pulley attached to the fork of the tripod. Four horses were hitched to a water tank which supplied water for the engine. Other items of interest in the picture are the lady riding side-wise on a man's saddle and a barrel for drinking water built on a two-wheel buck. Courtesy of Robert Beale

Fig. 111. Threshing methods in the 1890s. This threshing outfit used a donkey engine and a straw carrier instead of a blower. Two Jackson forks were used to move the headings from stacks to derrick table. The operator of the loaded fork, on the table, is holding the lanyard, standing near the sack pile. He was ready to trip the fork. A second man was starting another fork load. These forks were pulled with two horses each. One team is standing to the left of the table. The hoedown men were standing on the table to the rear of the loaded fork. Courtesy of J. W. Martin.

Fig. 112. Donkey engine and half moon separator. This engine is mounted on wheels. The straw is carried from the separator by means of an elevator as shown on the extreme left. The mouth of elevator moves from left to right, forming a half-moon shaped stack.

Fig. 113. Stack thresher. Headed wheat was stacked in ricks, which were stacks about 60 feet long, 15 feet wide and 12 feet high. The maximum number of ricks per stackyard was 12, because no more than that could be reached with the equipment. Six ricks were stacked in groups of three, with the ends facing each other. There was space between the ends of the two sets for a 12-foot derrick table. Another set of six ricks was placed about 60 feet away, parallel to the first six. The space between was for the separator and other equipment. All 12 ricks were threshed from the first setting of the separator and engine. After the first six were threshed, the derrick table was moved to the opposite side of the separator. These ricks were stacked with ordinary pitchforks. The 12 ricks could yield about 2,500 sacks or 6,000 bushels. If the grain has been stacked with a derrick instead of pitchforks, all 12 ricks could have been included into two large stacks. This operation generally used about 30 horses and 25 men. Straw fueled the steam engine. One man hauled water with a team of six horses. Most of the original outfits had two water wagons. One was left with the engine at all times. Hodgins Drug Photo, Moscow, Idaho

Fig. 114. Steam-powered thresher ready to move. The fact that the feeder is folded beneath the front of the separator is evidence that this was a separator for threshing bundles. We also know the engine used wood or coal for fuel because there is no straw wagon shown in the picture. This combination of equipment made it possible to move the separator without horses, which was unusual for steam power. Bill Walters Photo

Fig. 115. Harvesting with bundles. The binder was developed soon after McCormick invented the reaper. This was a logical improvement, since the reaper collected the sheathes in bunches. The headers and combines were developed to harvest crops of big acreages grown on steep slopes. However, there were areas of high rainfalls and heavy morning dews in which the crops did not mature until late autumn. Also, many of the varieties grown at that time retained moisture in the stems after the heads matured. To contend with these conditions, the push-binder with a 12-foot sickle bar was developed. If the grain was cut with binders, it was tied in bundles and placed in shocks throughout the field. Shocks contained from 5 to 12 bundles which were set with the heads up. A bundle thresher used a separator with band cutters attached to the feeders. The bundles were loaded into wagons hauled to the separator and then hand-pitched into the feeder. This eliminated the derrick table, Jackson forks and men (hoedowns) for pulling the headings into the feeder, for operating the Jackson fork and for driving the derrick team. Two horses pulled the bundle wagon. The wagons pictured here did not have a wide rear axle-tree or a high left side, but many did.

Fig. 116. Bundle threshing near Steptoe Butte, Washington. This bundle-threshing system was operated with a steam engine and four bundle wagons. Only two horses were used to pull each bundle wagon. This area is relatively level and the bundle racks were small, built on a narrow rear axle. A wide axle was always used in areas of steep slopes. This picture shows a typical sack-sewing system used by all stationary threshers. The sewers faced each other on each side of the sackjig, who is standing in front of the sacker. The sacksewers' seats were made of two filled sacks — one atop the other. The filled sacks were piled in tiers of five sacks high, as shown in lower right of the picture. The sacker has been extended with an overhead trough, so that the bundle wagons may drive near the bundle feeder.

Fig. 117. Threshing equipment for headings. This separator was equipped with a derrick for unloading headings. Nets were used to move the headings from header boxes to derrick table.

105

Fig. 118. Three 4-horse wheat teams. Each wagon was hauling 40 or 45 sacks of wheat. They were not using neckyokes or breeching harnesses on wheel teams. Each 2-horse team was pulling direct from the load. There were no eveners between teams in tandem. These teams were the property of S. M. Yadon, Bluestem, Washington, September 4, 1914. Courtesy of Richard Walter

Fig. 119. Loaded wheat wagons at the end of their trip. As soon as the wheat was harvested and sacked, it was hauled to the nearest railroad station and placed in a warehouse. These teams and wagons were waiting their turn to unload. Teams of four, six or eight horses were used. The general practice was to hitch wheat wagon teams in tandem of twos. This eliminated problems of passing on narrow, winding roads. However, some drivers hitched their teams in tandem of fours. All wheat wagons were pulled with a modified "dead hitch". They used 2 and 4-horse eveners with each evener being hitched direct to the wagon. There were no eveners between tandems of either of the 2 or 4-horse teams. Wagon beds were 16 feet long and would hold as many as 60 sacks. Forty or 45 sacks were considered to be the maximum load for four horses. A 60-sack load required six horses. If more than 60 sacks were hauled with a team, two wagons were hitched in tandem. Courtesy of Richard Walter

109

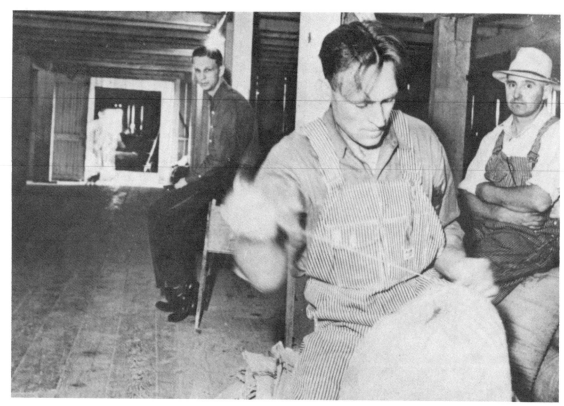

Fig. 120. W. C. Loney sews a sack of wheat. In a contest in 1937, W. C. Loney placed seventh in jigging and sewing, first in plowing, eighth in fencing, first in bundle shocking, fourth in hay pitching, third in harnessing and hitching a team, first in sack bucking and first in tractor driving.

Fig. 121. 2-horse wheat load. A combine dropped five or six sacks in rows at certain convenient loading areas. The 130-pound sacks were picked up in quantities of five to 20 sacks by a small wagon or a stoneboat and hauled to a convenient wagon-loading site. This wagon is loaded with 25 sacks at the Oglesby ranch, Peck, Idaho, 1911. Courtesy of Gainford W. Mix

Fig. 122. Hydraulic pump. Each tank was equipped with a hydraulic hand pump with a capacity of about two barrels per minute. Joe Dvorak Photo

Fig. 123. Loading a boat, before 1883, Lewiston, Idaho. The greater part of the wheat of Whitman County was loaded on boats at Lewiston and Almota, Washington, before the railroad reached Colfax. A tramway was constructed on the Washington side of the Snake River for moving wheat sacks from the top of the breaks to the river boats at Lewiston. Courtesy of Clifford M. Ott

Fig. 124. Theodore Roosevelt and Wheat. Sacks of wheat were used to build a platform at the entrance of the Administration Building, University of Idaho, Moscow, Idaho, for a campaign speech of Teddy Roosevelt in 1911. Courtesy of the University of Idaho Library

Fig. 125. Outside storage of wheat, 1912. A "bumper" wheat crop in 1912 made it necessary to stack wheat sacks in an open area without cover. This was before the development of elevators operated by gasoline engines. The sacks were lifted to the top of the pile with cable and pulleys and a horse. Courtesy of the Library of the Washington State University, Pullman, Washington

112

Fig. 126. Outside storage, showing equipment and method of stacking wheat sacks. Courtesy of C. M. Ott

Fig. 127. Outside storage, showing method of arranging sacks to ensure stability of the sack pile. Courtesy of C. M. Ott

Fig. 128. Bumper crop in 1937 in Adams County, Washington. Whenever a bumper crop occurred, it was necessary to store the overflow on the ground outside of the warehouse. This photo shows the method of constructing a rick of sacks to insure stability, and safety and to prevent any loss. A wood platform was constructed to eliminate dampness and furnish a level floor. The wheat sacks were overlapped, as shown in the end of the pile, to insure a tight, stable stack. Courtesy of C. W. Ott

Fig. 129. Method of storing sacks inside the warehouse. Interesting to note here are the methods of loading the handtruck and the procedure for elevating grain sacks. Courtesy of C. W. Ott

114

Fig. 130. Unloading wheat wagons at the railroad wheat station. Courtesy of C. W. Ott

Fig. 131. A fly trap. A fly-catcher was commonly used in or around the cook wagon of a stationary thresher. The cone-shaped screen within and fastened at the bottom of the screen cage had a hole at its top. The cage was placed over a pan of sweetened water. After the fly enjoys a drink, he naturally flies upward through the hole in the tip of the cone, where he becomes a prisoner. Pioneer Museum Village in Fort Walla Walla Park. Ross Watson Photo, 1971

Fig. 132. The thresherman's dining hall. A house on wheels, called the "cook wagon," was always located within 30 or 50 yards of the threshing operation — on the windward side. The house was generally 16 to 18 feet long and 10 feet wide. It contained a wood or coal cook stove, a cabinet for storage, ice box and small 4' x 4' tables. Space was available for seating 25 to 40 men at one time. Two or three women were used for preparation of meals. A man with four horses was assigned the task of moving the "cook wagon" when the thresher moved. All heavy duties about the house were the responsibility of the men. Breakfast was served at 3 A.M., lunch at 9 A.M., dinner at 12 noon, lunch at 4 P.M., and supper at 8 P.M. This cook wagon from the Jim Robinson ranch near Walla Walla, Washington, is now located at Pioneer Museum Village in Fort Walla Walla Park. Carl Penner, in charge of the museum (left); William Loney (right). Ross Watson Photo, 1971

Fig. 133. A steam engine. This was a typical steam engine for the period between 1900 to 1910. It had tremendous belt power for the operation of machinery — especially grain separators — but very little drawbar power. The drive belt wheel is shown just above the traction wheel. A steam whistle is just above the drive belt wheel and the top of the governor's to the right of the whistle. A fine-mesh wire screen covers the smoke stack for restricting fire sparks. Straw was generally used as fuel. This engine is on exhibit in the Pioneer Museum Village in Fort Walla Walla Park. Ross Watson Photo, 1971

Fig. 134. Jackson, harpoon and hoedown forks. Each of these forks had a specific purpose. The small one with a long handle (held by W. C. Loney on the right) was called a hoedown. It was used to pull the headings into a feeder from a derrick table. The feeder carried the headings to the cylinder of the separator. The 6-tine Jackson fork which I am measuring (left) was used to move the headings from the stack to the derrick table. This fork was fastened to a cable pulled by two horses. The gadget sitting between the two Jackson forks was used to move hay from a wagon. The 4-tine Jackson fork was used to lift hay for barn storage and stacks. These are in the Pioneer Museum Village in Fort Walla Walla Park. Ross Watson Photo

Fig. 135. McCormick header with header box, 1921. The header was the machine most commonly used for harvesting in the steep hills of the Palouse area. This header was operating near Mockonema, Washington. It was owned by my father, A. N. Keith. I am the header puncher. Eight horses were used to push the header and four pulled each header box. In the photo, the empty header box had pulled under the elevator (spout). If the hills were not too steep, the loader climbed on the top of the elevator during a change of boxes. He began loading the front portion of the box, where he put the butts of the straw in an upright position. He finished loading the rear right-hand corner of the box.

Fig. 136. Front view of a header and four header-boxes. This picture shows the position of the header puncher during the harvesting operation. He is standing on the rudder platform (at the end of the beam); this was the center of draft and was about two feet to the left of the bull-wheel (front view). Four horses were hitched on the left side of the beam (front view) to the rear of the sickle, platform and reel and four were hitched to the rear of the spout and header-box. The driver of the header-box had to regulate the location of the header-spout so as to have the box loaded uniformly from front to rear.

118

Part Five
THE HEADER

The header originated from a modification of the reaper. When the length of the sickle-bar of the reaper was increased for the purpose of increasing the width of the swath, the operation was not successful because of side draft. The side draft was easily eliminated by hitching the horses in the rear of the reaper where they pushed instead of pulled. The push machine was called a header because it could be manipulated to cut only enough straw to collect the heads of the wheat plant.

HOW THE HEADER OPERATED

The header was designed specifically to cut all heads of the grain crop so they might be delivered to a thresher or be stacked for threshing at a later date. The length of the straw cut varied with the height of crop and the variations in contour of the land being cut. Under most conditions, six to 20 inches of straw were cut. Twelve inches was the most desirable length.

The header was a three-wheeled machine, pushed instead of pulled. By pushing the machine instead of pulling it, the team was kept from trampling down the uncut grain on steep slopes. Pushing also eliminated side draft.

The three wheels were called the bull wheel, the grain wheel, and the rudder. The bull wheel was about eight inches wide and four feet high with heavy steel lugs about six inches apart. These were set diagonally across the tire. A large sprocket wheel was attached to the hub for the fitting of a heavy sprocket chain called the bull chain. The bull chain supplied the power to operate the sickle, reel, and all drapers.

The grain wheel was made of steel with a tire about four inches wide. Its purpose was to carry the platform and reel of the header. The rudder wheel, made of solid cast iron, was about two and one-half feet high with a concave-shaped tire. The concave tire gave the grappling power for guiding the header.

Most headers cut a 14-foot swath. A few had a 12-foot cut. Some were modified for cutting a 16-foot swath.

An elevator called the spout was attached to the left end of the platform and was used for elevating the heads to a header wagon. The spout was attached to the platform with a gadget which gave a hinge type of movement. This permitted the lifting and lowering of the mouth of the spout for adjustment to the side of the header wagon.

A rope and a set of pulleys were used to regulate the height of the mouth of the spout. One pulley was attached to the frame of the header. The other was attached to the upper part of the mouth of the spout. The header puncher had complete control of the rope. It was attached to the lever at the jacob staff.

An endless draper made of canvas and wooden slats was attached to rollers on the platform in rear of the sickle for collecting the heads and transferring them to the spout to be elevated into the header wagon. The spout had two endless drapers, one on top side and one on bottom side, to carry the heads upward.

HEADER PUNCHER

The "header puncher" was the driver of the horses that pushed the header. A header puncher had to be alert, strong, agile, and quick to understand the physical endurance of his horses. Since he was in full command of the operation, he had to be aware of the temperament and capabilities of the box drivers and the header box loader.

Header punching was an easy assignment when cutting gentle slopes of 10⁰ to 30⁰ with a crop of uniform height and a soil without deep water ditches and badger holes.

It was necessary for the puncher to stand while the header was in operation. There was never any time for sitting. The puncher stood on a cast iron platform about 30 inches in diameter. Many of the platforms had a part of the right and left sides tilted to give the puncher a place to brace his feet on steep slopes. This platform, being cast iron, would become extremely warm for his feet during the hot part of the day. Under conditions of continuous use and hot weather, the platform

119

Fig. 137. Rear view of header and header box, 1910. The angle of single trees shows the steepness of the slope. The horse header hitch with the 4-horse eveners is shown just to the rear of the horses. The header puncher has his right hand on the handle of the level used to adjust the height of the sickle for cutting the straw. The header-box loader is standing to the rear of the spout. The box driver is standing in front of the spout. Bertha Anderson Stipe Photo

Fig. 138. Loaded header-box. This box had been loaded and the loader had climbed to the top of the spout. You will note that the headings are not trampled and the cut ends (butts) are tightly packed in upward position. This prevented shattering and tangling of the straws. The load could be unloaded by nets or slings or it could be pitched off by hand. Bertha Anderson Stipe Photo

120

became slippery. A sheepskin tied over the platform contributed to a cool, safe footing.

An experienced puncher in excellent physical condition could operate a header without undue exertion and fatigue. Cutting grain on steep, soft slopes required considerable effort, however. When the header was in operation and cutting grain, the puncher stood on the rudder platform with full control of four lines and the lever that determined the length of straw cut. The ends of the lines were tied to the top of the jacob staff.

The puncher controlled the direction of the header with a 4-inch board that extended forward from the steel staff attached to the fork of the rudder wheel. This board was between his legs, about three inches above his knees.

Since it was important that the header cut a full swath at all times, the puncher had to watch the header box team and consider their degree of fatigue. Cutting grain down a steep grade required the use of a brake to regulate the speed.

LABOR AND ITS PROBLEMS

Naturally, the purpose of developing machinery to be operated with large numbers of horses was to reduce manual labor. Labor needs for soil preparation and seeding were easily supplied by permanent residents; extra labor was needed during harvest.

One man and eight horses could handle all the field work required to farm 320 acres. Three men could fulfill the labor needs of an area ranging between 600 to 1,000 acres.

During harvest if a header cut the grain and the headings were stacked without a derrick, the operation took eight men 12 days and another 25 men three days to thresh a crop from 320 acres. This required approximately 1,000 men to harvest a township. A total of 10,000 transient labors would pass through a town like Colfax, Washington. These transients supplied labor for approximately 10 townships, assuming that about one-third of the land was being summer-fallowed each year.

The source and training of these transients was especially interesting. They were men of about every experience conceivable. Many had traveled in numerous parts of the world. A few had completed college. As would be expected, a high percentage spent their earnings in saloons.

Most of these workers spent their winter months in Southern California or similar areas. They moved north as the wheat ripened. Many completed their yearly harvest in British Columbia or Alberta, Canada. Their source of transportation was the freight train.

The actual major labor problem was not the large numbers involved, but the human relationship involved with finding an individual who could handle an assignment efficiently and would remain on the job until the work was finished.

The problems were not involved with strikes or sabotage by labor organizations as was publicized by some fiction writers. It was true that labor organizations existed, the most common being "The Industrial Workers of the World" (IWW). It was possibly true that many fires were set by dissatisfied workers. Very few, if any, were reported to be of the IWW organization.

Zane Grey's book entitled "The Desert of Wheat"[1] would lead one to believe that the IWW's, as an organization were burning wheat fields, barns, homes, and threshers. Zane Grey's stories were strictly fiction and were written without his having seen the West. I have seen and experienced fires of all types, but have never known of one to be started by organized labor. I have seen many fires started as a result of smut explosions. On the final day of threshing in August, 1923, I counted 13 fires within a radius of 20 miles. These were reported to be due to smut explosions. Very few of these threshers were burned because the operators had learned that by tossing dirt into the separator as soon as it exploded, the fire was blown on out.

Fig. 139. Rear view of header and header-box, 1910. Frank Schrieber was the owner of this harvesting equipment which included the header, four header-boxes and a stationary thresher. Lee Hubbard was the header-puncher. I am the driver of the header-box. The slope of the hill clearly demonstrates the need for the box to have a high left side and a wide rear axle. Bertha Anderson Stipe Photo

Fig. 140. Too steep for the horseless machine. The area shown in this picture is located near the Whitman County fairgrounds on Highway 95 about a mile from Mockonema, Washington (see map page 16, section 19, township 16, range 43 east). At present, the slopes near the top of the hill are considered too steep for cultivation with modern horseless machinery. I had the assignment of punching a header over this area when I was 18. At that time, every foot of the area was farmed. The contour of the land was different from the usual surroundings in that the hills were not long and high. They were small, steep and cone shaped. Since header wagons had a wide rear axle and a narrow front axle, a short turn of the team to the left was always downhill. This would upset the wagon on the hill in this picture. We had hired a lad of 16 years for a header-wagon driver. He had been a telegraph boy in Spokane, Washington, and had never driven horses before. He was an only child and his father had passed away several years before. This was on his fifteenth day of driving, we were harvesting in this steep area. We made a special effort to instruct him in detail on every situation. So far, we had not had a tip-over. During the previous year, the heading crew had had one per day. On this occasion, we had finished loading his wagon at the top of the hill shown in the picture. It was about 11 a.m. and everyone was thirsty and weary. There was a geodetic steel stake on top of the hill protected by three fence posts. The lad inquired, "What's that?" The loader of the header wagons answered, stating that it was a "blankety" monument for the "blankety" box drivers who had given their lives trying to harvest this "blankety" country. The lad responded, "I am going home to my mother." After the noon meal, he was taken to Colfax, Washington, enroute to Spokane. George Woodbury Photo, 1970

Fig. 141. Too steep for the horse. Presently uncultivated, the area along Highway 95 across Union Flat toward Dusty, Washington, was first planted to wheat in 1918. It was my first year of driving the header. While cutting the last swath near the top of this area, the upper horses moved a step up the slope and stopped. The hitch with checks and lines became so tight the team could not move. The header box loader climbed to the upper side and gave this horse a tremendous shove. This enabled the team to move off the steep slope and avoid a mix up. George Woodbury Photo, 1970

Fig. 142. A typical heading outfit. The most efficient method of harvesting wheat on the large angular hills which are common in Whitman County, Washington, was the header. In the low rainfall areas near Lacrosse, Pomeroy and Walla Walla, the header was especially popular. Since most of the varieties of wheat grown between 1900 and 1920 tended to shatter, harvesting with a binder was not practical in many areas. The combine had two big drawbacks: the difficulty of driving the big teams over the hills and the waste of straw which could be saved by stacking when the header was used. The picture shows the location of the mechanical parts of the header. The bull- wheel — the wheel that supplies the power that operates the sickle, drapers, and reel — is located to the rear of the draper platform (the left end, as seen by the driver). The grain-wheel is about four feet from the right end of the platform. The draft center of a header was about two feet to the right end of the bull-wheel. A hollow-iron beam, 4 inches in diameter, extending from the rudder wheel, was attached to the left end of the platform and could be adjusted for height at the upper end. The reel was twisted, when cutting long straw, to cause the buttends to fall first. This made it easier to load with the butts up. Courtesy of Bill Walters

123

Fig. 143. Thresher for 2 headers. To cut the grain crop at the time of threshing, a harvesting outfit with two or more headers was not uncommon. A steam engine was used to operate the separator during the early 1900s. Total number of horses and horses per hitch were:

8 header wagons	x 4 horses - 32	1 roustabout wagon	x 2 horses - 2
2 headers	x 8 horses - 16	1 derrick team	x 2 horses - 2
1 cookhouse	x 4 horses - 4	Total horses	60
1 water tank wagon	x 4 horses - 4		

The two headers could cut from 50 to 60 acres per day. Wheat yields ranged from 25 to 50 bushels per acre. A day's threshing could vary from 1250 to 3000 bushels, or 500 to 1400 sacks. This required two sack-sewers and a jig. Twenty-seven men were assigned as follows:

Separator mechanic	1	Sacksewers	2
Separator oilman	1	Sackjig	1
Engineer	1	Hoedown men	3
Fireman	1	Derrick driver	1
Water buck	1	Header punchers	2
Straw buck	1	Box loaders	2
Cookhouse roustabout	1	Box drivers	8
General roustabout	1	Total	27

Header wagons were unloaded with nets, which rolled the load over the high side of the header box onto the derrick table (see on right of photo). Courtesy of Bill Walters

Fig. 144. 6-horse header with four 2-horse header-wagons. Fourteen horses were used on this outfit to operate the header and header wagons. Level areas of central Washington could be harvested efficiently with fewer horses.

Fig. 145. Unloading boxes with jackson fork. A four-tined Jackson Fork is shown loaded with headings at the end of the boom. Header boxes were mounted on a wagon gear with narrow rear axles and pulled with two horses. The header has a 12-foot sickle bar and is pushed with six horses.

Fig. 146. Randolph header advertisement. The procedure for operating a header was greatly different throughout Kansas and nearby areas than in the Soft White Wheat area. The Midwest farms were smaller in acreage with no hills. Four horses pushed a ten foot header. Two horses would easily pull a header-box. Ross Watson Photo

Fig. 147. Two headers and a gas operated thresher. Here is a harvesting outfit that included two headers, a 20-40 Rumely Oil Pull engine and a Case separator. This system used eight header boxes with the two headers. Since the engine did not burn straw or use water, men and horses for hauling water and moving straw were not needed. Cars and pickup trucks hauled fuel oil for the engines. The total number of horses and horses per team were:

8 header wagons	x 4 horses - 32	1 derrick team	x 2 horses - 2
2 headers	x 8 horses - 16	Total	50
Nineteen men were assigned as follows:		Derrick driver	1
Separator mechanic	1	Header punchers	2
Engineer	1	Box loaders	2
Sack-sewers	2	Box drivers	8
Hoedown men	2		19

This outfit could cut and thresh the same acreage as a steam-operated thresher with 60 horses and 27 men. Courtesy of Bill Walters

Fig. 148. Header and thresher combination. A Rumely Oil-Pull, 16-30 engine and a 24-inch Case separator (owned by A. N. Keith, 1921) were used to thresh the crop as it was hauled from the header with header boxes. A 16-30 engine was once constructed with a 16-horsepower drawbar and 30-horsepower drive belt. The term "24-inch" referred to the width of the cylinder in the separator. This system of harvesting, which began about 1910, eliminated the burdensome task of stacking the headings and waiting for a thresher. Harvesting grain with a header and a thresher also eliminated a tremendous waste of grain. The goal of this system was to thresh each day as many bushels, as the header would cut. A 14-foot header could cut an average of 25 acres per day. Twenty-five acres at 60 bushels per acre would be 1,500 bushels or (1,500 x 60 pounds/bushel) 9,000 pounds of wheat threshed per day. Since there would be 130 to 140 pounds per sack, this could mean that the sacksewer would fill about 700 sacks per day. Filling and sewing 700 sacks by one man within 10 hours was more than a sack per minute. Very few men were physically capable of jigging, sewing, and stacking 700 sacks. Since the yield of the great portion of acreage harvested was about 30 bushels, the average day's work for a sacksewer was between three and four hundred sacks.

Fig. 149. Thresher crew. A 24-inch Case separator, owned by A. N. Keith in 1923, threshed wheat as it was cut by a 14-foot header. This operation required a harvesting crew of eight men — one header puncher, one box loader, four header box drivers, one spike pitcher and one mechanic who operated the engine and separator. The horse and labor expense were $110 per 10-hour day.

	Daily pay rate		
Header puncher	$ 15	Sacksewer	11
Separator and engine operator	20	Spike pitcher	7
Four box drivers @ $6 each	24	24 horses @ $1 each	24
Header wagon loader	9	Total	$110

Fig. 150. Harvesting crew, Sunday afternoon, 1910. This harvesting crew operated a combination header and thresher. The crew included a header puncher, a header box loader, four box drivers, two hoedowns, a sacksewer and a mechanic. The individual standing first on left is Frank Schrieber, owner of the outfit. I was a box driver and was standing fourth from the left. Bertha Anderson Stipe Photo

Fig. 151. Unloading boxes with slings. This heading outfit is equipped with a derrick for unloading header wagons and each header wagon is equipped with a rope net called a "sling." With the use of cables and pulleys, a team of horses would pick up the sling and transfer the load of headings to the stack. The sling was constructed in halves. When the load was lifted above the stack, the halves separated at the bottom of the load, leaving the headings on top of the stack.

Fig. 152. Early model pull-binder. This binder was made with a 4-foot cutting-bar or sickle. The tongue has been removed and a 2-wheeled truck was attached to carry the weight of the forepart of the binder. An exhibit in the Cottonwood Museum, Cottonwood, Idaho. Joe Dvorak Photo, 1971

Fig. 153. Two push binders in operation. These two push-binders were operated with six mules each. All push-binders were built with 12-foot sickles. If the sickles had been longer than 12 feet, the handle-tying apparatus could not have handled the extra straw; if shorter, there would not have been sufficient room for six mules or horses. The push-binder was an adaption of the pull-binder for harvesting cereal crops in areas where the hills were steep and the straw matured slowly. These binders were operated in the vicinity of Moscow, Idaho, where the varieties of wheat produced long straw and the straw did not mature as rapidly as the heads. If a header had been used to harvest the crop, the straw would have contained too much moisture to cure in a stack. Eight men were required to shock the grain harvested with these two push-binders. Hodgins Drug Store Photo

Fig. 154. Front view of a small pull-binder. This shows the bundle-tying mechanism, reel and sickle. Ross Watson Photos 1971

Fig. 155. Rear view of a pull-binder. The rear view of a pull-binder which is on exhibit in Pioneer Village at Fort Walla Walla. This photo shows the twine box and the bundle-tying mechanism. Joe Dvorak Photo, 1971

Fig. 156. Pull-Binder operated with power take-off. A six-foot pull-binder pulled and operated by a Farmall tractor. The binder is operated by a tumbling rod which extends from the tractor to the binder. The tumbling rod operates the sickle, drapers, reel and the bundle-tying attachment. Courtesy of Floyd W. Trail, Moscow, Idaho

Fig. 157. Bundle-thresher of 1915. This picture was taken in 1969, after the equipment was set up to demonstrate bundle threshing of the early 1900s. It is a Case separator with a vertical-fan blower used to remove the straw from the machine. The feeder of the bundle-separator was located parallel to the drive belt. The feeder draper was not operating. Tom Baker Photo, 1969

131

Fig. 158. Water tank and 6-horse team. A threshing operation had to be provided with water tanks. In the Soft White Wheat Area, there were many streams and springs with pure fresh water. However, sometimes it was necessary to haul a water tank a distance of two or three miles. Two water tanks were used. One tank was left with the steam engine while the other was being filled. Courtesy of Dave Ferguson.

Fig. 159. 4-horse wheat load. This is an excellent example of a loaded wheat wagon during the period 1900 and 1910. The wheat wagon was built with low wide-tired wheels. All sacks, except for 10 under the driver's seat, could be loaded by two men standing on the ground beside the wagons. This load contains 40 sacks. Bill Walters Photo

Part VI

THE IDAHO NATIONAL
HARVESTER

The "Idaho National Harvester" was a push-type combine manufactured at Moscow, Idaho, from 1905 to 1918. It was pushed, rather than pulled, and was designed especially for use on steep slopes.

Designed in 1904 by Cornelius Quesnell and A.M. Anderson, this wheat harvesting machine developed into one of the marvels of the soft white wheat area.[1] Quesnell and Anderson were granted a patent on their invention in 1905.

The inventors' cash was exhausted before they had perfected the machine, since they had only $1,000 to spend on the project. G.P. Mix, an implement dealer in Moscow, became convinced that there was merit to the harvester and he induced J.J. Day to advance the necessary cash to build a trial machine.

One hundred acres were combined with the first machine during the 1905 wheat harvest. The machine cut a four and one-half foot swath and required four horses and two men to operate. The cylinder and concave each were the same length as the sickle bar.

The 1905 combine was placed on the market for $700. At that time, the 16-foot combine cost $2,000 and its operation required 33 to 44 horses and at least five men.

The principle of the push-type combine was the same as that of the header and push-binder. The header and push-binder were designed to operate on steep slopes, with the horses stationed at the rear of the machine so that they did not trample the uncut grain.

The Idaho National Harvester, as built from 1906 to 1918, had an 8-foot sickle bar and an 8-foot cylinder. Six or eight horses were used to push the machine. Two men and eight horses or mules could harvest an average of 15 acres per day if the hills were not overly steep.

The 1908 machine weighed 2,240 pounds, as compared to the next lightest combine which weighed 22,000 pounds. It required 11 men one week to produce the 1909 model.

A glowing account of the public demand for the harvester appeared in an advertisement in *The Idaho Post,* Moscow, Idaho, on March 3, 1911. The advertisement stated that only 3,000 shares of $10 stock were left. The capacity of the plant was not large enough to meet the demands, it was said. A thousand machines could be disposed of within the next two years and the plant could not put out over one-fifth of this number during that time. All the money was invested in buildings and machinery with no debts. The buildings were all concrete, and the machinery all iron and steel. The profit on 1,000 machines would be $50,000. Since there were 10,000 shares, a dividend of five dollars per share was anticipated.[2]

The Idaho National Harvester owned 12 different patents in the United States and one in Canada.[3] Among these were a draper equalized cutting device, a corrugated threshing tooth, a special length of cylinder, a tilting device, a tractor wheel pneumatic separator, a self-leveling sickle bar, and a pitman drive. The corrugated threshing tooth had 10 times the threshing surface at a lower speed than that of an ordinary tooth. The pneumatic separator contributed to an even distribution of wind pressure.

In 1912, Russia became interested in the machine for use in the wheat fields of southeastern Russia. At that time, the U.S. government had abrogated its commercial treaties with Russia. In spite of this difficulty, Russia persisted in requesting permission to use the machine.[4]

The factory was unable to meet the market demand of 10 to 20 machines per day for the 1912 model. Two machines per day were the limit of production.[5] A total of 52 machines of this model were sold during the year. The machines were priced at $1,100 each.

Wheat growers in Arizona and California were interested in the 1916 model. Arizona growers ordered six machines.[6] Two of the Idaho Harvesters were credited with some unusual

CORNELIUS QUESNELL
INVENTOR

ANDREW M. ANDERSON
INVENTOR

The first machine built in 1905, was
a 4½ ft. cut and run with 4 horses.
This machine cut and threshed several sacks. It gave the inventors the
encouragement out of which has developed the greatest harvester of the
age.

Fig. 160. Cornelius Quesnell and Andrew M. Anderson, inventors of the "Idaho National Harvester".

Fig. 161. Horses and side view of an Idaho harvester, 1911. Four horses are hitched on each side of the beam. Two men operate the machine on level ground — one man drives the team while the other fills and sews the sacks. The bull-wheel supplies all the power for the operation of the sickle, reel, drapers, cylinder, and for cleaning of the wheat. Ed Snow, Moscow, Idaho, owner and operator. Courtesy of the Library of the University of Idaho

134

records in harvesting wheat. A machine purchased by W. H. and F. E. Carpenter of Florence, Arizona, cut 600 acres in a period of 32 days. This machine was operated by Frank Gale. Another Arizona man, William Weimerskirch, cut 723 acres with his combine. It was another record for a season. Calculated in dollars, the advantages of the Idaho Harvester over the older methods of harvesting netted the Arizona owners a big saving — enough to pay the entire cost of the first machine during the first year of its operation plus some $300 to $400 surplus in addition.

In 1918, the orders for the Idaho National Harvester included 11 carloads to California; five carloads to Walla Walla, Washington; four carloads to Grangeville, Idaho; two carloads to Vollmer and one carload to Hyham, Montana. Each train carried three complete machines. The company built no more combines after 1918.

The Idaho National Harvester property, located on North Main Street in Moscow, Idaho, was sold to the Engineering College of the University of Idaho, in October of 1923 at a price of $45,000. This included six acres with buildings providing 2,000 square feet of floor space.[7]

WHEN HORSES AND MULES PUSHED

Horses and mules moved headers, push binders, and push combines such as the Idaho Harvester up, around, and over the hills of the Palouse country during the horse era of soft white wheat production. They were hitched in the rear of the machines. One of these machines could be seen for approximately every 640 acres of wheat.

This performance was almost unbelievable, from the standpoint of people from wheat growing sections of other parts of the United States or abroad. Of the three machines, the header was the most common one used. The header was more adaptable to wheat harvesting for all areas, especially the low rainfall sections. The binder was not used in areas of low rainfall where the growth was sparse. Under these conditions, the kernels were easily shattered while the bundles were being tied and tossed on the ground.

The header was a modification of the reaper specifically designed to cut the grain plant at a height to include 18 to 30 inches of straw with the heads. This made it convenient for delivery to the thresher or to be stacked for threshing — and the headings could be handled without an excessive loss of the kernels.

The header was a three-wheeled machine having the bull, grain, and rudder wheels. The bull-wheel was about five feet high with a steel tire approximately eight inches wide with steel lugs attached diagonally across the face of the tire. A chain sprocket was attached to the hub of the wheel. An endless chain called the bull chain passed over the bull-wheel sprocket and a small sprocket which gave power to operate the sickle, reel and drapers. The drapers carried the wheat heads from the sickle through the elevator to the header box. The bull-wheel was located just to the rear of the left side of the sickle bar.

The rudder-wheel was made of solid steel about two feet high with a concave shaped tire. It was used to control the direction of the header and the concave tire gave it a firm grip on the straw-covered ground. The fork of the rudder-wheel was attached to a solid steel pipe about five inches in diameter that extended from the axle of the bull and grain wheel. A square-shaped rod extended upward from the rudder-wheel fork through a swivel attachment on the rear of the header beam to a height of about the hips of the header puncher. A four-inch board was attached to the top of the square-shaped rod, extending forward about two feet. The header puncher stood on a metal platform with the rudder board about six inches above his knees and between his legs.

The header was built with a sickle bar of 12, 14, or 16 foot lengths.

The grain-wheel was located about four feet to the left of the right end of the sickle bar. The grain-wheel carried the right side of the header platform.

The push binder was a modification of the header with the bundle-tying attachment instead of the elevator. The push binder cut a 12-foot swath.

Basically, the Idaho Harvester was a header that combined the heading and threshing operations. It was called the push combine. It had an attachment that separated the grain from the straw and chaff instead of an elevator or a bundle-tying mechanism. The Idaho Harvester was first designed to cut four and one-half feet and used four horses. The late model had an eight-foot swath and used eight horses.

Fig. 162. Three Idaho harvesters, 1909. Twenty-four horses and six men would cut a total of 45 acres per day on a farm near Palouse, Washington. If the wheat yield averaged 40 bushels per acre, 800 sacks were filled each day. Drivers (punchers) of the machines are shown standing behind the jacob staff on a small metal platform. The ends of the lines are attached to the top of the jacob staff. The puncher has two lines in each hand. In addition to driving the horses and guiding the combine, the puncher adjusts the leveling mechanism for cutting the proper length of straw.

Fig. 163. An Idaho harvester approaching the corner. When the driver of a push combine approached a corner, he proceeded to crowd the four mules on the right of the beam toward the beam. This was necessary in order to turn the combine to the right. Courtesy of Gainford W. Mix

DUTIES OF THE DRIVERS OF THE MACHINE

The procedure and duties of the drivers of the three harvesting machines were not greatly different. The driver of the header was known as the "header puncher". The drivers of the Idaho Harvester and the push binder were called "punchers". Photos in this section show the puncher at work. He stood on a metal platform above the rudder wheel. The rudder could be used to vary the direction of the machine six feet or more without turning the team. In order to make a turn at an angle above 30 degrees, it was necessary to coordinate the team and rudder. In order to turn right, the teamster crowded his right four-horse team to the left — tight against the header beam. The left team of four horses was directed to the left at the same time and the rudder was pointed to the left as well. When the header reached the proper location for the turn, the team and rudder were directed forward again.

The other duties of the teamster (or puncher) were adjusting the height of the sickle bar and controlling the down-hill speed with the brake rope. In addition, he had to anticipate the problems of the box driver, watch the loader, and look out for signs that the box and header horses might be tiring plus always being on guard against any unusual incident that would interfere with the efficiency of operation.

It was necessary for him to stand and be alert to any irregularities of ground conditions, such as badger holes or ditches caused by water run off. The duties of a header puncher required a man who was strong, alert, and willing to take physical torture. There were times when on steep slopes of rough ditched-like ground, it was necessary that he hook his right foot and leg around the rudder staff to assure balance and safety.

The operation of the header was easy on slopes of 5 degrees to 30 degrees if the platform sloped from right to left and the headings were flowing downhill. The operation required considerable extra effort on level ground, on slopes greater than 30 degrees, or when the headings were elevated uphill.

Fig. 164. Procedure used in turning a push combine. The left-hand or swing team is directed to the left as soon as the machine has completely finished cutting the swath. The right-hand team is crowded toward the beam. Courtesy of Gainford W. Mix

Fig. 165. Completing the turn. A rear view of the position of the mules of both teams during process of turning the push combine. The driver directs the rudder to the left until the sickle and reel are in line with the uncut grain. Courtesy of Gainford W. Mix

Fig. 166. Turned and ready with full swath. As soon as the machine was in line with the grain, the left team was pulled to the beam. The right team was allowed to adjust to the right.

Fig. 167. This Idaho harvester required 12 horses. The extra four horses were required to operate on hilly ground. They were hitched in tandem of twos to avoid trampling the uncut crop. Four lines were used to drive the extra four horses. This picture gives a clear view of the size and construction of the bull-wheel. Courtesy of Gainford W. Mix

Fig. 168. This Idaho harvester used 11 horses. Heavy growth of straw and steep hills slowed the operation of the machinery. Three extra horses were required to keep the bull-wheel moving fast enough to prevent clogging of the cylinder. Courtesy of Gainford W. Mix

Fig. 169. Oxen and an Idaho harvester. Oxen proved to be a good source of power in Argentina. Collars, bridles, tugs and lines were the same as used for horses. Courtesy of Gainford W. Mix

Fig. 170. Rear view of the Idaho harvester and ox team. This scene was photographed in Argentina. Undoubtedly, trained sack sewers were not available, since the wheat-filled sacks were tied. Courtesy of Gainford W. Mix

Fig. 171. Idaho harvester converted to a pull combine. This Idaho harvester was converted to be pulled by a tractor. The beam, jacob-staff (for adjusting the height of the sickle) and the hitch were removed. Then the beam was attached to the front part of the bull-wheel for pulling the machine. A wheel with sprocket and chain was constructed above the right side of the reel to adjust the height of the sickle. This is the only Idaho harvester known to be intact. At present it is on display in the Lion's Club Museum at Cottonwood, Idaho. E. H. "Jack" Tackle is standing in front of the bull-wheel. Courtesy of Washington Water Power, Spokane, Washington

This combine called the Idaho Harvester was manufactured in Moscow, Idaho. The first such machine appeared on Camas Prairie in 1910. It took quite a little faith at that time for the pioneers to put their trust in a machine that would cut and thresh their grain at the same time. This machine is powered by a bull-wheel. (ground power) It took three men to operate the machine. It has an eight foot cut and cylinder. It was purchased by Rudolph Von Berge Fenn, in 1916 and used by him for many years.

Fig. 172. History of the Idaho harvester on display in the Lion's Club museum, Cottonwood, Idaho. Joe Dvorak Photo, 1971

Fig. 173. Pulling instead of pushing — Idaho harvester. Eight horses were pulling the 8-foot Idaho National Harvester originally constructed to be pushed. The beam used to push the combine was converted to a tongue. This was necessary for control of the direction of the machine. Courtesy of J. W. Martin

Fig. 174. Front view of an 8-horse team pulling the Idaho harvester. The disadvantage of pulling the Idaho Harvester was that the horses would be in the uncut grain when harvesting steep slopes. The height of the sickle-bar was adjusted with a lever located to the right of the driver. On the push-combine, the lever was located on the jacob-staff. Courtesy of J. W. Martin

Fig. 175. Freight cars loaded with Idaho harvesters. Idaho harvesters were shipped in large numbers to Arizona, California, and Argentina. Courtesy of Gainford W. Mix

Fig. 176. First home of the Idaho harvester. The first Idaho harvester was built in 1904 in this blacksmith shop on North Main street, Moscow, Idaho. Courtesy of Gainford W. Mix

Fig. 177. The second Idaho harvester building, 1906. Idaho harvesters were built in this building from 1906 to 1909. Courtesy of Gainford W. Mix

Fig. 178. Outside view of the Idaho National Harvester assembly building, 1911-1916. Courtesy of Gainford W. Mix

Fig. 179. Interior of the assembly building for the Idaho harvester, 1911 to 1918.

Fig. 180. Idaho harvesters in the process of being assembled. The semi-complete harvesters contain bull-wheels, grain-wheels, cylinder concaves, and separators. The reel, beam, rudder-wheel, and hitch have not been attached. Courtesy of Gainford W. Mix

Fig. 181. The cylinder of the Idaho harvester. The cylinder and concaves were of the same length as the sickle and reel — the first time this had been done. The same ratio is used in modern self-propelled combines. Before the Idaho Harvester, pull-type combines were built with narrow cylinders. The Idaho Harvester carried the crop to the front or face of the cylinder with a draper. Courtesy of Gainford W. Mix

146

Part Seven

GREAT HORSEMEN,
HORSEWOMEN,
AND HORSES

For both men and horses, harvesting work in the wheat fields was strenuous and demanding. The men working on the combine and header crews needed stamina and endurance in order to keep at their jobs day after day. Especially difficult was the job of driving big teams over hills and rough terrain. This was hard, grueling work — an assignment that often taxed to the fullest extent the driver's physical strength and his skills of horsemanship.

At this date, praise for the great horsemen and horsewomen of the soft white wheat area is long overdue. Consider the fact that in this area between 1900 and the introduction of horseless farming equipment in the late 1920s, there were produced more horsemen of outstanding caliber than in any other section of the world. Does this seem to be an immoderate claim? It is well to remember that skills of horsemanship had unique importance in the soft white wheat area. Where else in the world could there be found 1,000 teamsters, between the ages of 12 and 50 years, each of whom had the skills to drive 33 horses on a combine?

Without exaggerating, the figure of 1,000 teamsters can be multiplied a number of times. In the early 1900s, several thousands of combines were used to harvest wheat in the soft white wheat area of the Pacific Northwest. At the same time, the headers which were in use required fully as many teamsters as the combines. In know-how and ability, the drivers who "punched" headers had to be tops. And for every header, there were four header wagons — each requiring an expert teamster.

Most of the teamsters were home-grown talent. The typical wheat farmer would give his sons on-the-job training at an early age. In every farming community, skills of horsemanship were prized highly. A special affinity between man and horse developed throughout the area — and this was expressed in many ways, including rodeo-riding. Bruce Clinton has studied the records of rodeo competitions in the era previous to 1938 and he concludes that not less than 75 percent of the top bucking-horse riders came from the Pacific Northwest states and Canada.

This list of rodeo champions included Yakima Canutt, Jackson Sundown, Sam Fisher, Faye Huboard, Guy Lamb, R.H. (Hugh) Ryan, Bob Askins, Shark Irwin, Turk Greenough, Earle Thode, Harry Knight, Doll Aber, Nick Knight, and Floyd Stillings (the only man ever to win the New York Pitch-In twice in succession).

In breeding and training horses, people of the Pacific Northwest have made outstanding contributions. Altogether, the number of great horsemen and horsewomen from the soft white wheat area is so extensive that any listing must necessarily be incomplete. The people I tell about in the following pages have left their mark on history; they are achievers, people of distinction — and, yet, they are also representative of an area whose culture gave rise to many hundreds of people with exceptional skills of horsemanship. I am also noting the names of the horses which have special claim to prominence in the area's history.

YAKIMA CANUTT

Enos Edward Canutt, born and reared on a ranch at Penawawa, Washington, along the Snake River in the center of the soft white wheat area, was, in the opinion of his associates, the greatest horseman of all time. The nickname "Yakima" came during the 1920s when he was photographed while falling from a bronc. The reporters decided to call him "Yakima" and this became a permanent title.

In 1906, at the age of 11, he rode in the Border Days celebration at Grangeville, Idaho. He won the bronc riding contest of the Whitman County Fair at Colfax, Washington, and the Walla Walla County Fair at Walla Walla, Washington, in 1917.[2]

Fig. 182. Yakima Canutt receiving the Pendleton Round-Up Award, September 11, 1969. Courtesy of Howdyshell Photo, Pendleton, Oregon

148

The official record books at the Pendleton Round-Up, Pendleton, Oregon, show that Canutt won the all-around rodeo championship there in 1917, 1919, 1920, 1923, 1926, and 1928, which is more times than any other person in the history of the show to date. Canutt was all-around World's Champion Bronc Rider four times — 1917, 1919, 1920, and 1923.[2]

Canutt had the unique distinction of winning the Police Gazette Belt for the All-around Cowboy Championship three times, in 1917, 1919, and 1920. He won the Steer Bulldogging Championship in 1918, throwing two steers in 60 2/5 seconds and throwing one in 29 ½ seconds. He won the contest in 1920, downing two steers in 60 1/5 seconds, the best throw being 28 ½ seconds.[3]

Canutt was successful in riding the following horses: Smithy in 1915 whose record was 50 percent thrown, Old Colonial in 1916 whose record was 50 percent, "No Name" in 1917 who was officially known to have thrown over 1,000 riders, McKay in 1917 for 8 seconds, Corbett in 1917 for 16 seconds, and Culdesac in 1917 for 14 ½ seconds.[2]

Canutt is more famous for his work as a stunt man than for his early rodeo career. He was honored at the Academy Awards presentations in 1970 for his work as a stunt man.[2]

According to Charlton Heston[4] (who played the leading role in *Ben Hur*): "Ask any four men who was the greatest prize fighter and you're liable to get four different answers. The same is true in any discussion of the greatest author, football player, film director. But ask any stunt man who was the greatest in the stunt business and you will get only one answer: Yakima Canutt. He is also the greatest of the action directors for the simple reason he wrote the book."

Yakima Canutt directed the chariot race in *Ben Hur* and the battles in *El Cid*. He directed the horse action in *Khartoum, Ivanhoe, Helen of Troy, Knights of the Round Table, Song of Norway, Mogambo,* and *Fall of the Roman Empire*.

His ability as a horseman earned him acting roles in Hollywood. He starred in 48 five-reelers during the late 1920s. When opportunities as a straight actor appeared to be diminishing, he became interested in stunt work.

Again, according to Heston: "Before, stunt men were a disorganized bunch who would take a chance on anything. A lot of them got killed that way. Yakima came along and reduced stunt work to a science. He could do greater stunts than anyone else because he developed ways of doing them safely." Canutt's achievements are spoken of in reverent awe by the modern stunt men. He was the first to perfect the riding of a horse off the cliff into the water. In *Stagecoach*, he not only doubled for John Wayne but he also played the Indian who leaped on top of the racing team, then fell between the wheels of the coach. Once, he turned an Army tank over three times for a wartime film.

He turned to directing after snapping both ankles in a fall from a wagon for a Roy Rogers movie. He figured it was time to quit stunting. His first directing was in serials, then in low-budget Westerns. He was considered to be the authority on Western action movies. His first assignment for a big-budget movie came when he was sent to England to stage jousts and sieges for *Ivanhoe*.

From then on, he was in continuous demand as director of action sequences for big-budget epics like *Knights of the Round Table, Ben Hur,* and *El Cid*.

In many of these pictures, such as *Ben Hur, Khartoum, El Cid,* and the *Fall of the Roman Empire*, thousands of horses were used. Fortunately, Yakima had two sons, Joe and Edward, interested in and as adept at training horses as their father. Sometime before the start of a production, Yakima set up a horse training school with his sons in charge. They were experts at training the horses and men for falling in battle scenes. He and his sons have produced many battle scenes with as many as 30 horses and riders falling at the sound of a single shot — and those scenes achieved realism without injuring a single horse or man.[5]

At the present time, his sons are directing movie sequences concerning horses. Joe Canutt directed the action scenes for Heston's latest epic, *The War Lord*.

I knew Yakima when he was an active baseball player. He was a member of the Penawawa, Washington, baseball team at the age of about 15 years. The most common competitor was the Mockonema, Washington, team, of which I was a member. Naturally, I have followed Yakima's career with a great deal of interest.

DELL BLANCHETT

Dell Blanchett was the first recognized rodeo

Fig. 183. Yakima Canutt making a wild ride.

Fig. 184. Faye Hubbard and his 3-year-old Appaloosa stallion, Rex. This Appaloosa stallion owned by Faye Hubbard was bred by Sam Fisher. Rex, foaled in 1928, stood around 14-3 and weighed around 1050 pounds. People who attended rodeos in the Northwest during the 1930s remember this stallion as a versatile horse adapted to any duty a saddle horse could be used for. Courtesy of George Hatley

champion of the world. He owned and operated a rodeo circus that traveled to many countries, especially to those of South America, during the period from 1906 to 1912.

Dell and his wife, Bertha Blanchett, competed in the Pendleton Round-Up since its inception until he entered World War I. He joined the Canadian Calvary and was buried with other heroes under the poppies of Flanders Field.

FRANK HANNA

Frank Hanna was one of Yakima Canutt's early horsemanship teachers. Hanna owned a farm near Wilcox, Washington, where he built a race track to train chariot teams and running horses. He owned about 30 of the most attractive Percheron bred horses in the Northwest. The horses were used to operate a stationery thresher during harvest. He also owned and operated a cattle ranch in eastern Oregon.

SAM FISHER

Sam Fisher, a Palouse Indian, lived near Palouse Falls, at the mouth of the Palouse River. He produced many of the Appaloosas that became the foundation of present-day champions of the Appaloosa breed. Some of these were the stallion Rex and the mare Lucy, dam of Old Blue. Fisher lived to be 99 years old and died in 1945.

JACKSON SUNDOWN

Jackson Sundown, a nephew of Chief Joseph, was one of the top bucking-horse riders in the nation from 1912 to 1916.[6] He won the world's championship at the Pendleton Round-Up in 1916 at the age of 53 years. He became known as a top rider at the Grangeville Border Days Show in 1912. On the second day of the celebration, he rode a bull that the day before had sent a rider to the hospital in such bad condition that he was to be hospitalized for six months.

Sundown placed third in the Pendleton Round-Up in 1914 and second in 1915.

He was born in Montana in 1863 while his parents were with a band of Nez Perces from Wallowa County, looking for horses in the Flathead area. When he was 15, Sundown joined Chief Joseph's band in retreat into Montana during the closing days of the war of 1877.

ALLEN DRUMHELLER

Allen Drumheller, Walla Walla, Washington, was the son of an outstanding farmer, George Drumheller who owned and operated one of the largest wheat operations of the soft white wheat area. Allen was considered to be the peer of the relay riders and an all-around sportsman. He held the Pendleton Round-Up record in the pony express race until 1920.

The relay and pony express races commemorate the real-life races which cowboy mail carriers ran through the areas of hostile Indians. In both races, each rider has two assistants, one to hold and one to catch. Saddles must weigh at least 25 pounds with any type of cinch. Barring accidents, the same horses are to be used each day. The winner earns the best total time of the three-day contest. In the cowboys' relay contest, the rider has four horses. He must saddle, unsaddle, mount, and dismount unassisted, ride two miles each day, and change horses each half mile. On the first day, the riders draw for places in the paddock; afterwards, they take their places in the order in which they finish. Two times are assigned to each horse in the pony express and relay races.

Jessie Drumheller, a daughter of George Drumheller, was a splendid counterpart of her brother. She was a refined rider and was known as a superb relay rider. She held the 1918 girls' cowpony championship and also the record time (54 seconds) on the Pendleton track.

FAYE HUBBARD

Faye Hubbard was born and reared near Colfax, Washington. He won fame as one of the leading rodeo performers during the period between 1925 and 1940. He was the All-Around World's Performer in 1939 at the World's Fair in New York City.[12]

Faye married Kay Swift who had charge of the music and special entertainment of the fair. She was an author of a book (an autobiography) entitled *Who Could Ask for Anything More*. It was sold to RKO Pictures for $50,000. The title of the movie was *Never a Dull Moment*. Fred MacMurray played the role of Faye Hubbard and Irene Dunn played the role of Kay (Swift) Hubbard.

Faye and his wife Kay moved to Van Nuys, California, during the early 1940s where Faye did doubling and stunt work in Western movies. Faye rode an Appaloosa stallion named Old Res. This stallion was bred by Sam Fisher and was foaled in 1928.

Fig. 185. R. A. Long on a horse on the desert. "the ranch I have and the things I've done were due to horses." I had work horses for hire by contractors for freighting, haying, or construction jobs; I owned riding and pack horses for running dude outfits in the mountain; I raised riding horses to sell; I supplied bucking horses for rodeos; I broke horses for hire or just for fun; I caught wild horses and drove them in bands to the railroad; I bought and sold horses, hoping to make a profit; I kept horses for people short of pasture. A couple of times I rented horses and horse gear to movies. I am a horse-made man. There aren't too many persons in Oregon so horse diversified." Jackman E. R. and R. A. Long, *The Oregon Desert,* p. 16, 1965

Fig. 186. Floyd Hickman with an offspring of Toby I at his ranch at Almota, Washington. Courtesy of George Hatley

CECIL HENRY

Cecil Henry, reared in the soft white wheat area, began his rodeo career in the early 1920s. He participated in the major rodeos of Canada (including the Calgary Stampede), London, Paris, and Australia. He rode many times in Madison Square Garden, Boston Garden, the Cow Palace, the Pendleton Round-Up, and the rodeo in Lewiston, Idaho. As a rider, he challenged a long list of outstanding bucking-horses — including Home Brew, Badger Mountain, and Midnight. He was known as "the cowboy with the million dollar personality" and retired in 1954.

CARL P. PENNER
HORSEMAN, FARMER, AND INVENTOR

Carl P. Penner at one time owned 120 horses. He farmed with a number of 3-bottom plows using 10 horses on each, five 40-foot harrows with eight horses per harrow, and three 33-horse combines. With this horse-operated equipment, he farmed 5,000 acres of leased land four miles from Starbuck, Washington, for 15 years. His biggest crop was harvested in 1927, from 3,000 acres. From 1932 to 1938, he purchased a total of 2,240 acres near Starbuck and Dayton, Washington.

Since his retirement from farming, he has been collecting horse-drawn farm equipment for the establishment of a museum on the grounds of the old Army fort at Walla Walla. Carl and his wife have contributed $25,000 to the museum to build an agricultural machinery building. In this building is a 20-foot pull combine completely equipped for operation with a 33-horse hitch. They commissioned an artist to make 33 life-sized mules which are harnessed and hitched to the combine.

A greater portion of the repairs and lost parts for the old farm machinery are made in his blacksmith shop. He has rebuilt several combine hitches, combines, headers, separators, and binders for the museum.

Penner has been recognized on several occasions. He was chosen to be Grand Marshal of the 1970 Southeastern Washington Fair and Frontier Days. In 1969, he was chosen Washington State's outstanding senior citizen for the "community beautification personal service award program" by Governor Dan Evans.

Penner has numerous inventions to his credit. These include a program of speeding of the traffic through the Panama Canal, an all-electric automatic automobile parking plan known as "pigeon hole parking," a lift that goes on the front of tractors and trucks for unloading, and a quick freezer that was used widely by the government in ships during World War II. He also developed the longest project in the world — the white stripes on the sides of highways that are used to promote highway safety in every state in the nation and in several foreign countries.

FLOYD HICKMAN

The late Floyd Hickman produced over 300 Appaloosas during the period between 1920 and 1950.

Hickman was born and reared on a cattle and wheat ranch near Almota, Washington. Although not trained in the basic sciences of livestock improvement, he had an unusual practical insight for selecting and mating certain horses for desirable characteristics. He enjoyed selecting and matching horses of good conformation and specific color patterns.

One of his accomplishments that gave him considerable pride was the selection and matching of eight pinto horses as an eight-in-hand team for Ringling Brothers Circus.

His greatest contribution was the matings that produced the Toby family. More outstanding Appaloosas can be traced to Toby I than any other stallion.

Hickman's contribution may be shown by the following matings:

$$
\text{Toby II}
\begin{cases}
\text{Toby I}
\begin{cases}
\text{Old Blue}
\begin{cases}
\text{Little Dan}
\begin{cases}
\text{Knobby}\\
\text{Spot}
\end{cases}\\
\text{Lucy}
\end{cases}\\
\text{Trixie}
\end{cases}\\
\text{Dapple}
\end{cases}
$$

The origin of the Toby family began in the early 1920s when Floyd Hickman rode 40 miles down the Snake River to Central Ferry, Washington, to breed an Appaloosa mare to a well-known Appaloosa stallion named Knobby. The stallion was owned by Chet Lamb. Hickman's Appaloosa mare was a red roan nam-

Fig. 187. Toby II. Toby II was bred, raised and trained by Floyd Hickman at Almota, Washington. The progeny of Toby II are present in every corner of the United States. He sired many of the outstanding registered mares of the Appaloosa breed, among them being Patch, Black Beauty, Princess Pat, Nahahuli Wahine and Tobee Anna. Tobee Anna was an outstanding cutting mare, one of the few trained for that purpose. Among stallions, Toby II sired Toby Patch, Chief Handprint, Chief Eagle, Genesee Chief, Toby III, Yakima Toby, Topachy, Kenny's Chief, Dolls' Boy, Polkadott Toby, Toby K and Toby II's Patchy. Toby II was purchased by George B. Hatley. He died as the result of an accident at the age of 23. Courtesy of George B. Hatley

Fig. 188. A branding sequence. George B. Hatley is standing in the center of the picture. Courtesy of George B. Hatley

ed Spot. This mating produced a stud named Dan. He proved to be an excellent foundation sire. He was black in front with patches on his white loin and hips. Dan weighed between 950 and 1,000 pounds and stood around 14-3 hands. He was an excellent stock horse.

Hickman's second great sire was Old Blue, a son of Dan and a mare named Lucy that he had purchased from Sam Fisher. Lucy was a red roan Appaloosa that stood around 15-1 and weighed around 1,100.

Old Blue was used more widely as a sire than any other of Floyd Hickman's stallions. Old Blue was black with white over loins and hips and later turned blue in front. At maturity he stood about 15-2 and weighed 1,100. He was undoubtedly the most popular stallion in the Palouse country, judging from the demand of his service. During one year, Old Blue stood to 109 mares outside his own band with credit for over 77 foals.

The third outstanding stallion in Floyd Hickman's program was Toby I. He was a dark blue roan with black spots over the loin and hips. He stood 15-2 and weighed around 1,100 pounds. He was sired by Old Blue in about 1935 and was out of an Appaloosa mare named Trixie. Trixie was a dark red roan in front, white with chestnut spots over the loin and hips. She weighed 1,050, standing 15-1. She was a race mare. She had speed and a fast start and was raced in many relay races in the Northwest.

GEORGE B. HATLEY

George B. Hatley,[8] executive secretary of the Appaloosa Horse Club, Moscow, Idaho, is one of the few men of whom it can be said: "He was the architect of a breed of livestock." His work to establish the Appaloosa breed has been extremely successful.

In 1946, he was appointed assistant secretary of the Appaloosa Horse Club. He became executive secretary in 1947. The office, with its records, was moved to Moscow, Idaho, at that time. Hatley started the *Appaloosa News* in 1946 and served as editor from 1946 to 1966. In 1947, he published the first Appaloosa Stud Book; in 1949, he produced and managed the first National Appaloosa Horse Show; in 1950, he co-authored the book, *The Appaloosa Horse*. He has written more than 100 articles, pamphlets, and bulletins on horses and range management. Hatley supervised the production of several

movies on horses. He has lectured and conducted seminars at universities and before horse groups throughout the nation.

In 1963, Hatley was honored for his contribution to the livestock industry with his picture being placed in the "Hall of Fame" at Washington State University. In 1971, he was given "The Distinguished Equine Award" at a Horse Science School held at Southwest Missouri State College, Springfield, Missouri.

George B. Hatley was born near Pullman, Washington, July 18, 1924. He attended a one-room country grade school, graduated from Moscow High School, and was awarded a B.S. degree from the University of Idaho. He served in the U.S. Navy during World War II.

Hatley purchased his first Appaloosa stallion in 1941. This animal was the 113th Appaloosa registered in the Appaloosa Club and George Hatley received club membership number 45.

PHIL COX

Horses were a major interest of Phil Cox, a pioneer settler in the soft white wheat area. He established a farm three miles from Hay Station, 34 miles from Colfax, Washington, in 1880. The 9,000-acre Cox estate was called the Cherrydale Stock Farm. Cherrydale Farm was formerly a sheep herder's range, Cox converted it to the most noted horse breeder's farm in the Inland Empire.

The ranch extended four miles north and south and three miles east and west, extending to within two and one-half miles of the Snake River. The ranch was located in a beautiful valley, called Alkali Flat, which was half a mile wide with a sparkling stream fed by numerous springs along its course. There was an ample supply of water for both man and animal the entire year.

Cox owned 140 head of Percheron horses, mostly purebreds and colts entitled to be registered. He bought a purebred black Percheron stallion from O.T. Thissler of Chapman, Kansas. Later he purchased from Thissler another noted stallion called "Diamond Dick." Diamond Dick produced colts weighing 1,550 pounds as two-year-olds. Cox produced 40 to 50 foals annually.

Offspring from these stallions and mares were too large for wheat farming. However, the logging industry required heavy horses and most of the geldings were sold to loggers in the areas of Potlatch and Bovill, Idaho.

Fig. 189. Toby I and Toby II. Toby I (left, in photo), sire of Toby II, was the champion performance horse at the first National Appaloosa Show held in Lewiston, Idaho in 1948. He won the parade class at Washington State University Open Horse Show at age 19. At the age of 22, he placed third in the Appaloosa Regional Show at Sandpoint, Idaho. Mrs. W. C. Racicot purchased him in 1954. He died at the age of 31 years. George B. Hatley was riding Toby II. Courtesy of George B. Hatley

Fig. 190. Toby II and George B. Hatley. Courtesy of George B. Hatley

In addition to horses, the ranch produced many other farm products. The area was ideal for fruit trees. Eleven acres were in Bing cherries. Because of the cherry orchard, the farm was named "Cherrydale." There was also a long row of 1,100 peach trees. In one particular year, Cox planted 600 acres of wheat, 400 acres to corn for hogs, and 35 acres to alfalfa. He also owned 400 head of hogs, a cross of the Poland China and Duroc breeds. He kept 150 hens and 22 stands of bees. Eventually, the farm was converted to an all-wheat operation and mules replaced the horses for farm power.

OUTSTANDING HORSEWOMEN

The story of "The Horse Interlude" would not be complete without a resume of the contribution of the women of that era. In the soft white wheat area, women's role with horses was restricted to rodeo riding and cow pony activities on the ranch. Driving teams for the plow, the drill, and the harvesting machine was not woman's work. Only on occasion would a few women be seen driving plows and wagons. I have never observed a woman driving a combine or header. In rodeo activities, women found dramatic and entertaining outlets for their skills with horses.[14]

In rodeo, the activities of women were restricted mostly to pony racing, relay horse racing, and standing racing. Occasionally, a few women participated in bronc riding and calf roping.

Names of horsewomen who starred at the Pendleton Round-Up were Bertha Blanchett, Katie Canutt, Jessie Drumheller, Mabel Strickland, Ella Lazinka, Vera Maginnis, Donna Card, and Lorena Trickey.

The rules of participation were the same for women as for men, with the exception of pony relay racing. Pendleton was the first contest which required girls to change their own saddles. However, they did compromise a little by allowing women a "drop" stirrup — a heavy leather strap below the stirrup to enable them to mount more easily — because the relay takes a great amount of endurance.

Bertha Blanchett entered the women's pony relay game six different years. She won two first world's championships. She completed in six consecutive years in the girls' standing race with a marvelous record of five world championships. She held the record in the cowgirls' relay race with three firsts, two seconds, and two thirds.

Bertha Blanchett was considered to be one of the greatest all-around range women America has produced. She had the remarkable distinction in 1916 of having come within one point of winning the all-around championship on both cowboys' and cowgirls' points — and would have won, had not one of her horses in the relay race jumped the fence. In 1904, she not only rode the famous bucking horse Dynamite at Cheyenne, but at Calgary drew and rode the wicked animal Red Wing which killed Joe Lemare.

When Bertha Blanchett's father took all of the docile horses away to prevent his little seven year old from riding them, she learned to handle and ride horses by capturing wild colts and riding milk cows nearly to death. In rodeo, she was an active participant in cow pony standing race at Pendleton. She competed in six consecutive years in girls' standing race and won five world championships, being defeated only once by Vera Maginnis.

Bertha Blanchett and Lucille Mulhall were top ranking experts in the game of the lasso rope. It mattered little to them whether it was fancy roping, lassoing an "outlaw", or roping and hogtying a steer. They handled their ropes as true champions.

KITTIE WILKINS

For many years, newspapers across the country gave frequent reports about Miss Kittie Wilkins of Glenns Ferry, Idaho. She was an outstanding rancher and dealer in horses. Wherever she travelled on her business trips, the local newspapers were sure to receive word that "The Horse Queen of Idaho" was in town. Colorful news stories about this remarkable woman were likely to result because Kittie Wilkins liked to talk with reporters and explain how her father helped her get started in the horse business and how her $40 starting capital was built into a fortune.

Born in Oregon in 1857, she moved to Bruneau with her parents in 1880. For more than 40 years, she and her father and her brother operated the Wilkins Island ranch near Bruneau. Kittie Wilkins was an expert horseman and continued riding for most of her life. She died in 1936.

Kittie Wilkins raised many riding horses and Clydesdales as well. She was well known by horse buyers throughout the nation. In one deal, she disposed of 500 animals. She sold many horses to the United States Cavalry.

157

Fig. 191. Start of the cowgirls relay race, Pendleton Roundup.

Fig. 192. Katie Canutt, winner lady bronco contest, Pendleton Round-Up, 1918.

In an interview with a San Francisco reporter in 1927, Miss Wilkins said: "I have been referred to as the 'cattle queen' but this is incorrect. The Wilkins Company of Idaho owns both horses and cattle, and this is how the mistake originated, but my own specialty is horses. I own between 700 and 800 of my own.

"It was real romantic the way I got my start. The way of it was this: My parents had moved to Oregon and were returning to San Francisco, when our friends gathered to give us momentoes of various sorts. When they got to me they said, 'Well, now, she's only a little thing.' I was but two years old. 'We'll give her some money to be invested for her.' Two of them gave me a $20 gold piece each. Shortly after, my father concluded to go to Idaho and engage in the stock business. He went to Oregon and bought a lot of horses. When he went to pay over the money, he thought about my $40, and seeing a young filly yet left, he offered $40 for her. The owner valued her at $80, but seeing that my father was taking the others, he finally concluded to let this one go, even if it was worth much more. From the increase, all my bands have come."

NO NAME

"No Name," a bronco who was known to be one of the most difficult horses to ride, was foaled in 1901 and began a conventional life pulling a buggy. When he was seven years old, standing 15 hands and weighing 1,200 pounds, he was used in small shows in Western Canadian rodeos and tossed any one who got on him. "No Name" had his name changed three times to fool the bronc riders. Many knew they could not ride him and if they drew him in the contest, they would turn him out.

In 1919, at Calgary, Canada, he threw some of the best riders, including Yakima Canutt and Jack Fretz. This attracted the attention of the officials of the Pendleton Round-Up, who purchased him for $1,000 for a bucking horse and shipped him to Oregon for the Pendleton show.

The four bronc riders who were successful in riding "No Name" were Yakima Canutt, 1917; Hugh Strickland, 1920; Ray Bell, 1922; and Bob Askins, who twice rode "No Name," once to a championship in 1925.

"EPIC DRAMA OF THE WEST"[13]
The Round-Up
Pendleton, Oregon
September, 1929

An Historical Event

On September 18, 19, 20 and 21, 1929, Pendleton, Oregon, will present its 20th Annual Round-Up. This event, staged annually by the community, serves as a monument in pageantry to the daring and gallantry of those sturdy pioneers who made possible the winning of the West and the subsequent settlement of the Oregon territory. This great outdoor pageant, setting forth the feats of strength, courage, and skill which marked the development of this Western country, is in its true sense "The Epic Drama of the West."

The first Round-Up was presented in the year 1910. Since that time it has grown to be the outstanding event of the great Northwest. There has been perfected an entertainment which is a credit to those sturdy pioneers who won the West, embracing the sports and pastimes which they enjoyed. It is community owned and community staged, rendering it free from commercialism and the selfish desires of professional promotors. It depicts an era of Western history that is as important to this great outdoor country as the landing of the Pilgrims is to those situated on the Atlantic coast.

The Opinion of an Educator of Note

The historic importance of the Round-Up was ably expressed by the late P.L. Campbell, president of the University of Oregon, who said, "I believe that it needs only to be more widely known to hold as significant a place in relation to history as do the major European festivals and community plays that attract visitors from all over the world." After declaring the Round-Up "a pageant unequaled for sincerity, proportion, and genuine beauty," President Campbell said, "Right back of the Round-Up is the whole history of American frontier civilization. Into it go the lives of three generations, and they are mighty important generations of American history. It is not a stunt. It is a pageant and a very beautiful, dignified and sincere pageant, springing from the united effort and pride of a community ... The greatest surprise to me was the beauty of the whole festival. It was the art that conceals art ... It has saved the historical and

Fig. 193. Kittie Wilkins, horse queen of Idaho. Courtesy of Idaho Historical Society

symbolical value and created of this seemingly unlikely material a real work of art."

World's Largest Indian Gathering

During the four days of the Round-Up a large and picturesque Indian village springs into existence on the Round-Up grounds. The tepees present an interesting and attractive picture, depicting the real American in his native surroundings. Over 1500 Indians participate in the daily parades and events, adding a natural color that is genuine in every respect. At no later place in the world can there be found this number of Indians clad in their finest raiment and wearing the legacies of many generations. Every brilliant color imaginable is represented to their make-up and the blending of these colors in the soft sunlight of September creates a picture that has every appearance of nature's own handiwork.

There are Indians in the Walla Walla, Cayuse, Umatilla, Nez Perce, Bannock and Yakima tribes. Entire families participate in the parades; the old warriors bedecked with the long flowing head dress and other marks of their station, the squaws wearing robes literally covered with precious elk's teeth, and the young braves unclothed save for a breech clout and unadorned save for a smear of hideous war paint upon their bodies and possibly an eagle feather in their straight black hair. Many of the young Indian mothers have strapped to their backs a tekash in which will be observed a serious-faced papoose, serenely observing the surroundings.

The Indians have acquired many of the white man's ways, and the Round-Up proves no exception to the rule. Entire families vie with one another in bedecking themselves in a more elaborate manner than their Indian neighbors. This rivalry is unique in that it furnishes an abundance of color and rich trappings which never make their appearance except at Round-Up time.

Contests Thrilling

The numerous events for which the Round-Up is noted include bucking, bulldogging, roping, and cowboy relay and pony express races. These events are under the strict supervision of the management, and all are contests — not exhibitions. The contests are thrilling and display a brand of horsemanship that can only be found in the West.

The relay and pony express races show the modern age the manner in which express and mail were transported at the greatest speed possible during frontier days. The quick changing of horses and saddles, the pony express mount, with departure from their station on a dead run clearly demonstrate the skill of the rider and the intelligence of his mounts.

In the bucking contests the skill of the rider is pitted against the skill of the horse, the latter emerging victorious in the majority of the events.

Steer roping demonstrates the skill with which a steer can be thrown and hog-tied for branding purposes, as is practiced on the cattle ranches yet in existence.

In bulldogging, human strength and skill are opposed by the animal strength and shrewdness of the steer. It is in reality a wrestling bout, in which the contestant usually receives the worst of the bargain. Excitement reigns supreme at the instant the rider leaves his horse, alighting on the run and grasping the steer by the neck or horns in an effort to stop the animal and throw him according to the strict humane rules adopted by the Association.

They are indeed contests of the most exciting nature, in which nothing but clean sportsmanship is displayed.

Happy Canyon

During the evenings of the Round-Up there is presented a gorgeous pageant depicting the coming of the white man to this Western empire. This is staged and controlled by the community under the auspices of the Chamber of Commerce. It is called the Happy Canyon Show. In the staging of this important event, recognition is given the American Indian to the extent that some five hundred full-blooded members of Northwest Indian tribes participate in a most colorful pageant that causes one to regret "the passing of the red man."

After the pageant Happy Canyon takes on the appearance of an old frontier town, the crowd assembling in an old Western dance hall, where numerous games of chance of the old West are provided in which the visitor can participate in a harmless manner.

The Happy Canyon Show is staged by business men who devote time and effort from their own pursuits; all amateurs, notwithstanding that the show itself would indicate the work and effort of professionals. It provides a medium of entertainment that will not permit the evening hours to become dull to our thousands of visitors and forms an appropriate ending of a perfect day.

Fig. 194. Walter Whitten, at the Pendleton Round-up, 1918.

Fig. 195. Stage coach race, round-up at Toppenish, Washington.

A Modern City

Pendleton, Oregon, is a modern city, but during the four days of each year the bustle of today meets with the easy progress of yesterday. It is a city of splendid environment and cultural advantages, whose citizens, true to the Shakespearean theory, provide a background that inspires every visitor to become a part, and a very important part, of this great annual pageant.

Transportation and Accommodations

Pendleton is reached via the Union Pacific System and the Northern Pacific Railway, and by two great highways, the Old Oregon Trail-Columbia River Highway and the Oregon-Washington Highway.

Ample accommodations are provided at the hotels, rooming houses, and private homes of its citizens, and the city maintains a modern auto camp accommodating approximately 600 cars.

A bureau is maintained by the Round-Up Association, the Round-Up acting as agent for the reservation of rooms in private homes at a stipulated price of $2.50 per night for a double bed and $1.50 per night for a single bed.

Round-Up grandstand seats, which are reserved, are $2.50 each per day. Bleacher seats, which are not reserved, are $1.50 each per day. Boxes containing eight seats can be purchased for the entire four days of the show or the last three days, at $96 and $72, respectively.

Tickets for the Happy Canyon night show, which are reserved, are $1.50 each per night.

We Invite You

The people of Pendleton and Oregon extend you a most cordial invitation to visit the twentieth annual Round-Up, September 18, to 21, inclusive, assuring you that every effort will be made to make your visit one of pleasure and interest.

Address all communications to The Round-Up, Pendleton, Oregon."

Fig. 196. Jess Stahl on "Grave Digger", Pendleton Round-Up, 1915.

Fig. 197. Catch-saddle-bridle race at the Pendleton Round-Up.

Fig. 198. Pendleton Round-Up parade, 1911.

Fig. 199. Round-Up parade, Pendleton, Oregon, 1911.

Fig. 200. Hitting the grandstand between the eyes, Pendleton Round-Up. "After the finish of the cowboys' and cowgirls' grand mounted march, this great horde of riders sweep across the arena in one tremendous stampede. Over the fence they rush, kicking the dust into the very lap of the grandstand as they bring up short under the very noses of the spectators in a wild, terrific climax of overwhelming numbers. Then as suddenly wheeling back, they retreat, disappearing through the gates in the gap toward the Indian village, and another thrill is marked in your diary." C. W. Furlong, in his book, *Let 'er Buck,* G. P. Putnam's Sons, the Knickerbocker Press, 1921

Fig. 201. The horse long gone. Remnants of the past — wagon running gear — add a note of nostalgia to this pasture scene. Here lie the rear axle tree with bolster attached, along with the detailed structure of a wheel. The hub, the attachment of spindle to axle tree, spokes, tire and tire rim are exhibited in detail. Since the spokes and wooden sections of the tire are shrunken by dehydration, the tire rim has slipped off. Dan Warren Photo

Fig. 202. First gas tractor. The first internal combustion tractor was built in 1892 by J. I. Case Co. It had a single cylinder with two large fly-wheels. Courtesy of J. I. Case Company

Part Eight

THE POST-HORSE ERA

The horse raises what the farmer eats, and eats what the farmer raises. But you can't plow in the ground and get gasoline—Will Rogers.

Perfection of the farm tractor took time. Engineers were working on these problems in the 1860s. During the next decade, the 1870s, farm traction steam engines were produced for sale by J.I. Case Co. and at least eight other U.S. firms.[1] It was not until the 1930s that the engineers had developed and refined the tractor to the point where it could consistently outperform horses.

The tractor has not drawn its power from renewable energy resources, as did the horse. This is a defect of modern mechanized agriculture which science must correct. As early as the 1930s the problem was recognized by agricultural researchers — including Hobart Beresford, then head of the Agricultural Engineering Department at the University of Idaho. Beresford in 1937 was advocating extensive research in the utilization of agricultural wastes so that "our agricultural industry will be prepared to contribute its share to our future motor fuel needs, when the present supply has been depleted to the extent that the need for national economy of our petroleum fuel resources becomes more apparent."[2]

It was home-grown feed that nourished the hard-working horses of the soft white wheat area. Perhaps the tractors of the area may someday be powered by home-grown fuel. Scientists of the Battelle Northwest Laboratories in Richland, Washington insist that with present-day technology huge amounts of methanol could be produced from the annual residues of wheat straw in the Pacific Northwest. Methanol, or "wood alcohol", can be used as a motor fuel or it can be converted easily into nitrogen fertilizer. Other waste products could be utilized as fuel also.

Looking into the future, it is possible to see dramatic changes coming to agriculture as new methods are initiated for generating and transmitting electric energy. The electric-powered agricultural implements of tomorrow could be totally unlike those in use in today's tractor technology.

BACK TO THE HORSE ERA?

At this time, even though an energy crisis exists, no one seriously suggests that American agriculture should return to the horse-powered technology of yesteryear. When this unlikely possibility is discussed, it is for the purpose of showing how difficult it would be to feed our nation with old-fashioned methods of crop production.

Earle E. Gavett, for example, says maintaining current U.S. agricultural output with the farming technology of 1918 would require 31 million farm workers instead of the 4 million presently employed.[3] Moreover, he estimates 61 million horses and mules would be needed to provide farm-power if existing farm tractors were retired from service. From his figures, it can be seen that Gavett thinks of horse farming in terms of two and three-horse teams — and a return to that state of affairs would indeed be intolerable. The situation would still be bad — although a shade less desperate — if farming were to be done with big teams of 16 to 43 horses. However, a revival of horse-farming practices is not likely to occur — not even in the soft white wheat area, where a high degree of efficiency was achieved with big teams in the past.

It is a fact of history that the big-team hitches which were used extensively in the Pacific Northwest did not find widespread acceptance in other farming areas. Attempts were made to introduce big-team farming into the Midwest and the Southwest. In fact, an ambitious campaign to promote big-team hitches was undertaken by The Horse Association of America in the early 1920s. The campaign continued for more than 10 years, with some encouragement and support from the U.S. Department of Agriculture and leading agricultural colleges.

This last-ditch effort to save horse farming was not successful. The tractor, despite its mechanical mysteries, often seemed not quite so perplexing to drive as were big teams of horses. Outside the

Fig. 203. An attempt to replace the horse. An Avery Truck with chain driven skeleton rear steel wheels was pulling a 3-bottom horse plow. Front wheels had solid rubber tires. Courtesy of J. W. Martin

Fig. 204. Case tractor, 1920s. Internal combustion engine using kerosene for fuel, pulling plows with independent trip beams. Courtesy of J. W. Martin

168

Pacific Northwest, horses and drivers were untrained in multiple-hitch operations. The entire principle of the multiple-hitch was foreign to many farmers' thinking. One agricultural engineer found midwest farmers confused by the problem of "aligning the center of the pull of the team with the center of resistance of the machine."[4]

The tractor's triumph over the horse became complete during World War II, when farm labor was in short supply throughout the nation. Farmers recognized the labor-saving advantages of mechanized farming and they were eager customers for whatever tractors were available. Nationwide, there was a big boom in tractor sales in the postwar period. Wheat farmers of the Pacific Northwest had been shifting to tractors in great numbers since the 1930s. Because the soft white wheat area had many hills, this was "caterpillar country" for many years. The track-type tractor could crawl over soft ground on steep slopes, while wheel-type tractors were less reliable under these conditions. With improved traction and design, the wheel-type tractors became more popular over the years.

SOIL CONSERVATION

Some of the problems of the future are going to be difficult to overcome, irrespective of what happens on the farm regarding new sources of power and technological developments. Soil conservation is one tremendously important problem with economic overtones. Even though the rich, fertile soil of the soft white wheat area was the region's greatest asset at the time man first cultivated it, this natural resource has never been protected adequately.

The soil scientists reported that the virgin soil contained large quantities of the essential plant nutrients — namely nitrogen, phosphoric acid, and potash. They, also, noted that the limiting nutrient was nitrogen and there was sufficient quantity to last 60 years of wheat production. This prediction proved to be accurate, since a fertilizer was not required until the early 1950s.

The present method of applying inorganic fertilizers and pulverizing the soil with modern machinery is without question contributing to a serious environmental situation.

WHEELWRIGHTING

Wheelwrighting is an ancient craft, known to few contemporary Americans. When the covered wagons moved westward on the Oregon Trail,

tools for repairing and rebuilding wheels were a necessary part of the wagon train's gear. Trained wheelwrights were available at the stop-over stations along the trail, and many conducted thriving businesses. During the horse era of wheat farming, as many as 48 wagon wheels were involved in a harvesting operation conducted with two headers and a thresher. Farmers of that era had to have the tools and know-how for repairing wagon wheels.

One of the few people who practice the craft of wheelwrighting today is Mel Dewitt, farm superintendent at the University of Idaho's College of Agriculture in Moscow. He has found it a very satisfying experience to master this almost-forgotten craft. If other Americans will explore our heritage of horse-related crafts, they are certain to find many opportunities for pleasurable hobbies and profitable avocations.

OUR HERITAGE INCLUDES PACKING[5]

You can't appreciate the skills which were associated with the horse era until you try to do some of the tasks the oldtime horsemen performed so well. Packing a horse is an example. This looks a lot easier than it is. If you want to learn the art of horse-packing, you will benefit from the instruction of an expert teacher. He will show you how to pack the cargo in pieces of light canvas called "mantees." For bulky, light-weight material, a mantee 7 by 8 feet may be used. A smaller mantee will accommodate heavier cargo. Always, the goal is to make sure that each pack which goes on the horse will be of equal weight.

The packer should be able to tie a variety of hitches. He has to have expertise in tying at least two — the crowfoot hitch and the post hitch. Cargo must be packed securely. And the packs have to be balanced — no small feat when you are packing with no scales at hand. The packer must be able to size up horses. The pack saddle will not ride well on a horse that does not have prominent, well-defined withers. Due to defects in temperament or constitution, some horses will be poor risks on the pack trail. Among other skills he needs, the packer has to develop old-fashioned "horse sense."

The United States Forest Service has been one of the largest users of pack animals. They were useful during the time that trails were being built and lookout towers were being established and supplied. The Forest Service still uses a large number of pack animals, although much of the fire lookout is done from airplanes now rather

Fig. 205. Trucking cattle in the early 1920s. This was an Avery chain drive truck with skeleton rear wheels, solid rubber tires and chain drive. Courtesy of J. W. Martin

Fig. 206. Skeleton wheel case tractor, pulling a horse mower, 1920s. Courtesy of J. W. Martin

170

than from lookout towers built on high mountaintops. At present, the largest users of pack animals are professional guides and outfitters who use pack strings for supplying hunting and fishing camps and for servicing tourists and sightseers who desire to take pack trips into scenic mountain areas.

Most of the early-day packing was done on a sawbuck pack saddle. The forks of the saddle were made of wood, and the cargo to be carried was packed in a rawhide or canvas box called a pannier or pack bag. These hung on either side of the saddle by a leather loop around the buck or fork of the saddle. Often more cargo was piled on the top of the saddle, a canvas pack cover would be put over it, and then everything lashed down with a diamond hitch.

During the Thunder Mountain gold rush, a packer named O.P. Robinette developed a pack saddle called the O.P.R. pack saddle. This pack saddle had rounded iron bars instead of wooden bars. A padded canvas boot covered the saddle and gave much added protection to the pack animal. Instead of the cargo being packed into a pannier, it was usually placed on a canvas called a mantee and then tied into a cargo or package. The cargo was tied on the pack saddle with a swing rope. The O.P.R. or Decker pack saddle proved to be an excellent piece of equipment for packing all kinds of unusually-shaped objects and freight ordinarily difficult to pack. This packing equipment gained in popularity and became widely used in the Northwest.

The pack animal moved the freight prior to wagons and roads. The pack animal still moves the freight in the roadless mountain and canyon country of the Northwest.

MACHINES, SHOES, AND WHEELS

These days, few people have the opportunity to get acquainted with the farm machinery our early-day farmers used. In this book, I have tried to explain both the machines and the functions performed by the header-punchers and the other experts who operated the machines. Anyone who wants to understand our agricultural heritage should study these machines at first hand. Some machines can be seen in local museums and private collections. There is a very fine display at Pioneer Village in Fort Walla Walla State Park, in Washington. The Idaho State Historical Society has plans for assembling a large exhibit of old farm machinery near Boise, at the site formerly occupied by the State Penitentiary. This exhibit

could possibly be one of the finest of its kind in the country. If funds become available, this projected museum will feature regular demonstrations of the old machinery in operation. This will be a great opportunity for people to see how hay was stacked and grain was threshed during the horse era.

Horseshoeing is an old craft which is much in demand, now that many people are owning horses for recreational purposes. The modern farrier often operates from a mobile shop — a well-equipped van. Some craftsmen operate over a wide area, travelling between horseshoeing assignments by airplane. The specialists in this line of activity, past and present, have gained renown for their ability to design shoes for special purposes and for horses with particular problems. This is a profession which should be attractive to young people who have brains, brawn, and the instinct of craftsmanship. Other people whose interests are historical may want to study old horseshoes.

Some horseshoes were made for exhibits and were signed by the proud craftsmen who created them. The University of Idaho College of Agriculture has an exhibit of horseshoes from the 1900-1920 period donated by Charles Staley of Spokane. Many of the shoes were signed by Staley. Others may have been the work of transient workers of that period. The name of Bob Fitzsimmons is printed on one shoe. Robert Prometheus Fitzsimmons died in 1917, some years after he gained fame in the boxing ring. This man, who held simultaneously the middleweight, light-heavy, and heavyweight championships of the world, was originally a blacksmith in New Zealand. How he happened to be in Spokane fashioning horseshoes for Staley is an intriguing topic for historical research.

RODEO, THE ALL-AMERICAN SPORT

The tradition of horsemanship remains strong in the Pacific Northwest. Here, the rough-and-tumble world of rodeo attracts large crowds of spectators and substantial numbers of local participants. Because rodeo is popular in most of the nation, the contestants who do well in small rodeos always have the chance of graduating to the big-time rodeo circuits and there attaining fame and fortune. Pushed on by the old American dream of success, rodeo stars exhibit the qualities of pluck and endurance to an amazing degree.

Fig. 207. New International Harvester plow. A semi-mounted plow plus trim snag-free beams is available with spring-trip beams in 3, 4, 5, and 6-bottom sizes. Courtesy of International Harvester Company

Fig. 208. 200 - horse power. The Steiger Super-Wildcat has a total weight of 17,000 pounds, is 228 inches in overall length and 105 inches in overall width. Equipped with 28.1 tires, this model was available with option of dozer, radio, air conditioner, swivel seat, 3-point hitch, and heater. Five six-horse teams which were used to pull five 10-foot grain drills would weigh approximately 39,000 pounds. Courtesy of David Anderson, Steiger Tractor Company

172

Fig. 209. Horseless farming of the 1970s. Here is Super Wildcat pulling 48 feet of grain drills which simultaneously seed and fertilize 30 acres per hour for an average of 300 acres per 10-hour day. Forty-eight feet of horse drawn drills would require at least 36 horses on the hills of the Palouse area and these teams would seed an average of about 140 acres per 10-hour day. Courtesy of David L. Anderson, Steiger Tractor Company

Fig. 210. A caterpillar pulled combine. This combine was of the same construction as the horse-pulled models, with sickle and reel on the left of the separator. The separator and header were operated by a gas engine. The Caterpillar tractor replaced horses during the early 1930s. This combination required a "Cat" driver, a header man and a mechanic. Courtesy of Roy Lundequist

Fig. 211. Two tractor-pulled combines. The reels and platforms are clearly shown. The platforms had an endless draper, carring the headings to the cylinders on the forepart of the separators. The widths of the cylinders and concaves were from 36 to 48 inches. Air-conditioned cabs, on the modern self-propelled combines, were unknown in this periods. Courtesy of Roy Lundequist

Fig. 212. Nine self-propelled combines. These combines, owned by Jim Hanson of Dixie, Washington, were doing custom cutting on the Omer Kent ranch at Eureka, Washington, in 1969. Photo by Bill Lilley, Walla Walla, Washington

Pacific Northwest rodeo performers have earned star status on the national scene. Jeff Copenhaver, the 1975 world champion calf roper, sometimes travels by chartered airplanes and helicopters in order to compete in two or three concurrent rodeos. He is the son of Deb Copenhaver, two times winner of the world saddle bronc championship. His father now lives in Creston, Washington.

Larry Edward Mahan of Brooks, Oregon, was the first man in history to win the World's All Around Rodeo Championship six times. This was two more winnings than those of Yakima Canutt and one more than Jim Shoulders.

Mahan completely dominated the World All Around Cowboy standings from 1966 to 1970. He returned after two seasons of injuries to capture the sixth title, along with the single season's high winnings record — a total of $64,446.

THE APPALOOSA IS REDISCOVERED

The Appaloosa breed of horses has had an important place in the history of the soft white wheat area. The Nez Perce Indians had impressive herds of spotted horses; they were the first Americans to be noted for breeding fine Appaloosas. After the dispersal of the Nez Perce herds, the breed seemed fated for extinction. Through the years, a few horsemen developed an interest in Appaloosas but their individual efforts were not unified through any organization. However, in recent years the Appaloosa breed has experienced a tremendous revival.

Organized effort — through the agency of the Appaloosa Horse Club — has revived the breed and given it worldwide prominence. The headquarters of the Appaloosa Horse Club is located in Moscow, a short distance from the campus of the University of Idaho. There is excellent cooperation between the University's animal scientists and the Appaloosa breeders.

In the past, the horse program of the University of Idaho College of Agriculture was concerned with the production of draft horses for agriculture. After tractor-farming became well established, the University discontinued its horse-breeding work and other horse-related projects. At present, the University's horse program is being revived — this time with an emphasis on light horses, principally Appaloosas. A breeding program, with Appaloosa mares and stallions, is projected. Instruction is to be offered in all phases of horse husbandry. For a

number of years, one of the most popular courses at the University has been a class in horsemanship.

In the field of research, University of Idaho animal scientists are beginning to probe the genetics of Appaloosa coat color. When the inheritance pattern of coat color is fully understood, Appaloosa breeders will be able to conduct breeding programs for the strengthening of desired colors.

APPALOOSA HORSE CLUB

The Appaloosa Horse Club was incorporated in 1938.[6] Interest in forming a breed association for Appaloosas was brought about by articles in *Western Horseman* written by Francis Haines. Francis Haines was working on his doctorate degree in history at the University of California when he found a statement written by Charles M. Russell, the noted Montana cowboy artist, about an incident involving a Nez Perce and an Appalousey horse. Since the Appaloosa was associated with the Nez Perce Indians and Dr. Haines was doing his work on the Nez Perce, he became very interested in the Appaloosa and did a great amount of research on this breed.

Claude J. Thompson of Moro, Oregon, one of the leading Appaloosa breeders at that time, did the actual organization and incorporation of the Appaloosa Horse Club. He wrote many articles about the Appaloosa which were published in livestock and horse magazines, and he also published an information pamphlet. Mr. Thompson was assisted by his two daughters Faye and Claudine.

George Hatley offered to help with registry work in 1946 and was appointed Assistant Secretary. He answered correspondence and put out a one-page mimeographed sheet called *Appaloosa News*. It was sent four times a year without charge to the members of the Appaloosa Club.

In 1947 George Hatley was appointed executive secretary of the Appaloosa Horse Club, and the records were moved to his home near Moscow, Idaho. The records were easily moved, as they were all contained in one shoe box. This included the membership list and the original applications for a little over 250 horses. In 1947 the first Appaloosa Horse Club Stud Book was published, and it listed 338 horses. The following year, 1948, the first National Appaloosa Horse Show was held at Lewiston, Idaho. It attracted

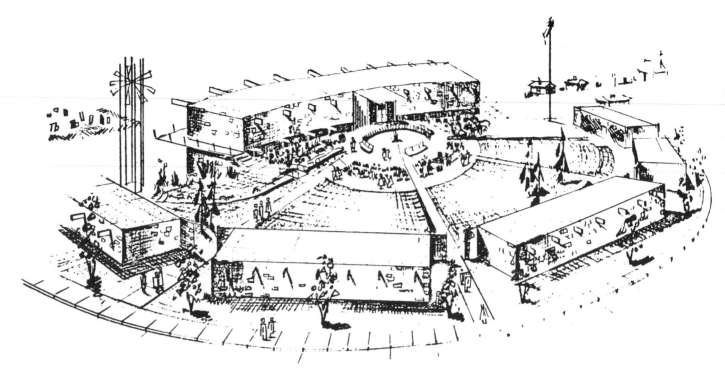

Fig. 213. Historical museum to be erected at Fort Walla Walla Park. Projected plans call for a 60 x 100-foot historical museum to be located on the edge of the hill overlooking the old Fort Walla Walla cemetery. Five implement storage buildings form a semi-circle surrounding the museum building. The over-all design resembles a broken-wagon-wheel with the museum being a part of the hub — while the implement storage buildings represent a section of the outer rim and the concrete walks extend from the hub to the rim to be the spokes. The museum will be two stories in height, an apartment for the caretaker being located on the lower floor. The space on the upper floor would be available for display purposes with meeting rooms. At the present time the area has combines, steam engines, separators, binders, wagons, furniture, early day kitchen furniture, and many other pioneer items. One implement storage building has been completed. It has a 33-horse combine which features the Schendoney hitch complete with single trees and harness for 33 mules. The mules are plastic replicas of an actual team.

Fig. 214. Fibre glass mules. Thirty-three plastic mules are shown to a combine in the historical museum at Fort Walla Walla Park. Carl Penner ordered the fibre glass mules for this historical exhibit. He obtained a model from southern California and arranged for the Alkirs company of Billings, Montana, to produce the mules from the model. The 33 mules cost $400 each, delivered to Walla Walla. Courtesy of *Ruralite,* Forest Grove, Oregon

Fig. 215. Self-propelled combine, upset. This is a Holt combine, showing caterpillar track (lower right), bull-wheel (upper right) and flanged steering wheel in lower left. Courtesy of C. W. Ott

Fig. 216. A self-propelled combine loading a truck in 1971. Wheat is cut, threshed and stored in a bin on the combine. When the bin is filled, the combine moves to a level area for unloading. Wheat of the horse-drawn combine was sacked and the sacks were placed in a carrier. After five or six sacks had accumulated on the carrier, they were dropped in a convenient area to be picked up by wagons or stoneboats. This picture was taken on the Don Hart ranch near Colfax, Washington. Courtesy of the *Spokesman Review,* Spokane, Washington, August 7, 1971

Fig. 217. Helping with the harvest, 1971. "Attesting to the abundance of the crop is Marcia Hart, 18, who helps drive trucks in the fields for her father, Don Hart, on the family ranch near Colfax, Washington." Courtesy of the *Spokesman Review,* Spokane, Washington, August 7, 1971

65 horses, mostly from the Northwest. This became an annual event. The first four National Shows were held at Lewiston, Idaho, and from that time on, they were moved to different parts of the country for the convenience of the owners in other areas and to help familiarize people with Appaloosas in other areas. The first National Appaloosa Sale was held in 1949 at Lewiston, Idaho, and it also became an annual event held in conjunction with the National Show.

By 1958, the Appaloosa Horse Club had outgrown the small farmhouse. George Hatley purchased a home at 820 East First Street that had a full basement that opened out onto the back lawn. The basement of the house provided adequate office space at that time. The staff was made up of George Hatley, his wife Iola, and one full-time stenographer. During the next five years, the work load increased to where the club had eight full-time employees and had outgrown the basement of the house on First Street.

In 1962, the Appaloosa Horse Club purchased a building at 403 South Jackson Street that was 40 feet by 125 feet. Initially, less than one-fourth of the building was used, and it appeared that the building would adequately house the registry for many years to come. By this time, the Appaloosa Horse Club had added a full-time field representative to its staff, and the breed publication *Appaloosa News* had grown from the one-page mimeographed sheet into a bi-monthly magazine, and then a monthly publication.

Interest in the Appaloosa was gradually spreading to all portions of the United States and regional Appaloosa clubs were being organized in all areas. The regional Appaloosa clubs sponsored horse shows, trail rides, parade groups, and many activities that served the needs of local Appaloosa owners.

By the mid-1960s, the Appaloosa Horse Club added a full-time editor for *Appaloosa News*, a director of racing, and a youth secretary to its staff. The number of registrations and transfers of ownership grew steadily, as did the equipment and the space required to store the records.

By the early 1970s, the building on South Jackson Street had been outgrown. In 1973, work was started on a new building one mile west of Moscow on the Pullman-Moscow Highway adjacent to the Washington-Idaho border. The building contains 17,500 square feet and is located on four acres of land. The records were moved into the new building in March of 1974. In addition to providing adequate space for both the registry and *Appaloosa News,* the building has one wing devoted entirely to the Appaloosa Museum. The museum shows Appaloosas in art from cave paintings to the present time. It also has exhibits of Nez Perce Indian regalia and utensils, a large contour map of the route taken by the Nez Perce during the Nez Perce War of 1877, equipment used by the cavalry during that era, equipment used by cowboys in the Northwest, and a large saddle collection. Also on exhibit are many of the early-day articles that were written about Appaloosas, the first three volumes of the Stud Book, early-day National Show programs, and some of the first issues of Appaloosa News. The museum is open to the public.

The Appaloosa has now grown to be the third largest breed in the United States. There are now over 40,000 members, over 125,000 owners and over 230,000 horses registered.

Fig. 218. 1971 Truck driver has time to read a line. Miss Hart waits for her truck to be loaded with grain. Her job allows for a few slack moments when she gets in a little reading while waiting for the combine to come again. Courtesy of the *Spokesman Review,* Spokane, Washington, August 7, 1971

Fig. 219. Outside wheat storage in 1971. Since there were no freight cars available during the 1971 longshoremen's strike, wheat soon filled the elevators and had to be stored in outside bins. These pictures were taken in August, 1971, at a wheat station near Pullman, Washington. After the elevator was filled, overflow was poured down the outside wall to a pen made of heavy lumber. This pen was about 60 yards wide and 400 yards long. Wheat was distributed throughout the pen by a fresno, which was controlled by a cable and windlass operated by electricity from a nearby tower. According to the Whitman County Agricultural Extension Agent, Felix M. Entenmann, 6 or 7 million bushels of the 12 million stored outside were damaged. Joe Dvorak Photo, 1971

Fig. 220. Construction of outside storage. The photo shows the type of construction of equipment used for outside storage of grain at Busby, a station near Pullman, Washington in 1971. Joe Dvorak Photo

Fig. 221. A big bin for outside storage. A large area was required for storage of surplus grain at Busby station near Pullman, Washington in 1971. Joe Dvorak Photo

Fig. 222. Modern method of unloading wheat. This truck will haul 55,000 pounds of wheat and can be unloaded in three minutes. Courtesy of the Spokesman-Review, Spokane, Washington

Fig. 223. Loading a truck from an elevator. Courtesy of Spokesman-Review, Spokane, Washington

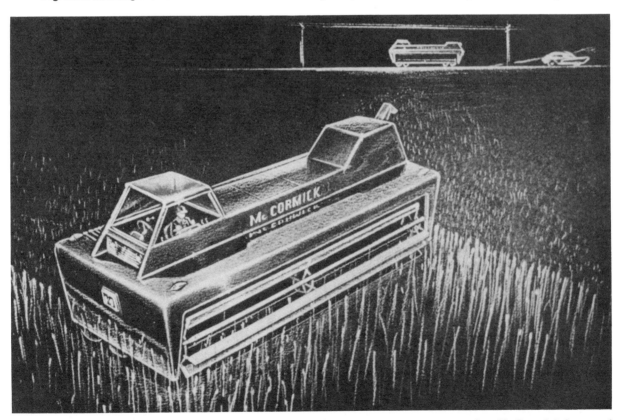

Fig. 224. McCormick harvester of the future. One hundred and twenty years after McCormick invented this reaper, an artist looks ahead to a machine that will travel 12 to 15 miles per hour, cutting a swath at least 20 feet wide, with the possibility of the grain being separated from the straw by centrifugal whirling chambers or by using a different electrostatic charge for the kernel than for the straw. The harvester could be constructed to be moved down the highway by pivoting the wheels and driver's seat 90 degrees. For complete automation, the harvester could be computer-operated without the presence of a man. Courtesy of International Harvester Co.

Fig. 225. Tractor with turbine engine. A tractor with a turbine engine would provide the future horsepower of the wheat farmer. As visualized by engineers, the tractor has the resemblance of a present day jeep, with air-conditioned cabin. It would weigh less per horsepower than tractors used in present operations. The extra horsepower of a turbine engine would permit a larger tractor to plow, cultivate, seed and apply fertilizers in one operation. With the engine placed under the control of a computer, the entire operation could be operated from the farmer's office. Courtesy of International Harvester Co.

Fig. 226. Soil erosion of 1965 in Latah County, Idaho. Many narrow deep channels were produced in the spring run-off of 1965. This field has been in alfalfa and grass most of the time during the past 10 years. Green manure was plowed under during the summer of 1964. The soil was worked deeply and left loose. Fall wheat growth was poor. During the spring approximately 200 tons per acre was lost from the steep slopes. Before 1920, during the era of the horse, heavy rains and melting snow did not produce deep ditches of this type. When horses were used instead of tractors there was not sufficient time to work the soil and pulverize it as farmers can do with modern machinery. Also, the soil of the early 1900s contained more humus, especially the north slopes of the hills. Ken Riersgard Photo, Courtesy of Richard J. Booby, Latah Soil Conservation District

Fig. 227. Retired wagon wheel. When the horse was replaced by the machine, wagon wheels were discarded and forgotten. This one was hung on a growing tree limb, as time passed, it became something of a novelty. It is now on display at Pioneer Village in Fort Walla Walla Park. Ross Watson Photo

Fig. 228. Wheelwright tools. Instructor M. L. DeWitt displays equipment and tools used in a wheelwright short course in the summer of 1975. He holds a tire bolt compressor "at least 75 years old." Other items are by number: 2 and 8, fire tongs; 3, ballpeen hammer; 4, grip tongs; 5, chisel; 6, chisel; 7, spoke shaver; 8, tongs; 8, hub unit; 10, spoke pointer; 11, draw knife; 12, traveler; 13, 14, 15, and 16, tenor auger; 14, brace and bit. Courtesy of Theodore E. Hoffman

185

Fig. 229. Rebuilding a wagon wheel. Edward Mahaffy and M. L. DeWitt installing new spokes. Courtesy of Theodore E. Hoffman

Fig. 230. Replacing a wagon wheel tire. Ray Nichols reconstructing a wagon wheel. Courtesy of Theodore E. Hoffman

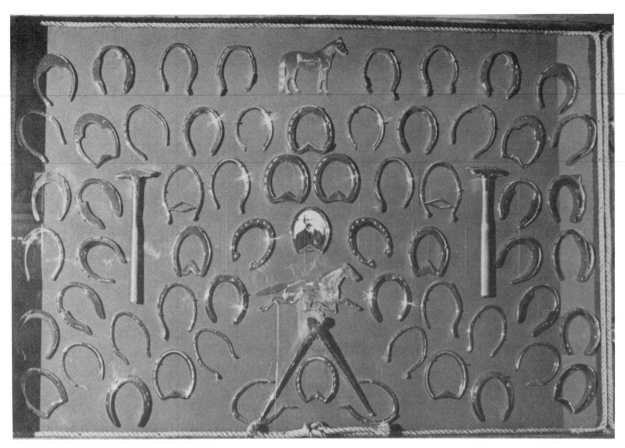

Fig. 231. Horse shoe display. This display of different types of shoes used for corrections of stride and gait problems of the horse was presented to E.J. Iddings, Dean of Agriculture, University of Idaho, during the late 1920s.

Fig. 232. Appaloosa Building, constructed in 1973, Moscow, Idaho.

Fig. 233. A modern packhorse. George B. Hatley is demonstrating a method of tying a pack. This pack saddle was designed by O. P. Robinette, an Idaho packer. Courtesy of George B. Hatley

Fig. 234. A mule pack team. The United States Forest Service maintains this pack team at Paradise Guard Station in the upper Selway of the Bitter Root National Forest. The mules are used for trail crews and camp packing. Courtesy of James M. Peek

Fig. 235. Appaloosa trail ride, 1975. Riders follow a good trail up a side draw that leads into Cottonwood Creek as they leave the campsite on the Lowell Grewell ranch in Southwest Montana. Each year since 1965, Appaloosa horsemen have retraced 100-mile segments of the Chief Joseph Trail. The rendezvous site for the 11th segment of the Appaloosa ride of the Chief Joseph Trail was near the mouth of the canyon of the Clark Fork of the Yellowstone on July 28, 1975. The first day's ride passed near Belfry, Montana, partly on or near the old Meeteetse Trail, an early-day stage route from Meeteetse, Wyoming, to Red Lodge, Montana. The second day's ride passed Bridger, Montana, where they camped on a branch of Bluewater Creek. For the third day, the riders rode through the area near Edgar, Fromberg and Silesia, Montana. The fourth day contined on through Laurel, Montana, following the blacktop highway north to the Canyon Creek Battlefield. The ride was terminated at the end of the fifth day along Canyon Creek. Courtesy of George B. Hatley

Fig. 236. Third day of the Appaloosa trail ride, 1975. Monica McDowell leads the riders to a crossing on Blue Water Creek and out to a long ridge that shows an excellent view of the country. Courtesy of George B. Hatley

Fig. 237. Fourth day of the Appaloosa trail ride, 1975. The riders splash through Canyon Creek for the benefit of the movie cameras. This picture was taken near the place where the Canyon Creek Battle started. Courtesy of George B. Hatley

191

Fig. 238. Daiquiri-Bar, champion Appaloosa mare. Twice winner of the National Appaloosa Halter Championship, this sorrel and white mare was donated in 1976 to the University of Idaho's Appaloosa horse program. Daiquiri-Bar was the gift of the Glen Hulcher family of Virden, Illinois.

Fig. 239. No longer a beast of burden. This Appaloosa is ridden by Carol Switzer, the horse's owner, in a bareback equitation class at the 27th National Appaloosa Horse Show, Shelbyville, Tennessee, June, 1975. Courtesy of George B. Hatley

THE HERITAGE OF THE HORSE

Throughout history, man and horse have had an intimate, but changing relationship. They were companions in hunting, travel, and various kinds of work and recreation long before the first horse-drawn plow was invented. Then, during their partnership as workers in the fields, they brought agriculture through many stages of technological development until mechanized farming became a reality. Horse farming has become out-of-date, but the horse will never be obsolete so long as people cherish this animal and prize its companionship. In a world that is becoming increasingly standardized and mechanized, the horse is a unique resource for recreational activities which can re-create within a person a sense of individuality and innovation.

The horse continues to play an important role in the soft white wheat area of the Inland Northwest. Here, before the coming of the white settlers in the 1850s, the native Americans took pride in owning and riding Appaloosa horses. For recreation, many present-day inhabitants of the area find great satisfaction in riding and training horses. The pleasure horse — symbolized by the beautiful Appaloosa — continues to enrich the area's way of life. The historical interlude in which tremendous agricultural progress was made with the multiple-hitch horse teams ended in the 1930s. In many families of the area, memories of the horse interlude remain very much alive.

193

BIBLIOGRAPHIC NOTES

Part One — PIONEER DAYS

1) Centennial Edition, Colfax, Washington, Gazette, July 13, 1972.

2) Kingston, C.S., Pioneer Roads of this Region. The Spokesman-Review, Spokane, Washington, July 1, 1957.

3) Information given to the author by a grandson of an owner of a group of covered wagons of the Oregon Trail.

4) Walter, Denny D., Largest Horse Raising Company in North America? Frontier Times 45: 35, 1971.

5) Haines, Francis, Red Eagles of the Northwest. The Scholarship Press. Portland, Oregon, 1939.

6) Drumheller, D.M. Tells Thrills of Western Trains in 1854. Inland American Printing Co., Spokane, Washington. 1925.

7) The American Anthropologists, Vol. XI, No. 3, p. 430 (July - September, 1939).

8) National Research Council. Pub. 1401. Nutrient Requirements of Horses No. 6, Washington, D.C., 1960.

9) Blaisdell, James P., A.C. Wiese and C.W. Hodgson, Variation in Cheminal Composition of Bluebunch grass, Arrowleaf, Balsamroot, and Associated Range Plants. J. Range Management, V. 5, No. 5, September, 1952.

10) Oregon Historical Quarterly, 18: 65, 1917.

11) Appaloosa is a Unique Horse Name, Idahonian, Moscow, Idaho, June 12, 1964.

12) Avery, Mary W., History and Government of the State of Washington. University of Washington Press, Seattle, 1961

Part Two — THE WHEAT HORSE

1) Millikan, Ben. S., The Greatest Invention Since the Wheel, Farmland News, Kansas City, Missouri. July 15, 1972.

2) Keith, T.B., The Mule and Wheat Farming, The Western Horseman, April, 1971.

Part Four — STATIONARY THRESHER

1) Dinge-MacGregor, Science of Successful Threshing, J.I. Case Company, Racine, Wisconsin, 1915.

2) Centennial Edition, Colfax Gazette, Colfax, Washington, July 13, 1972.

Part Five — THE HEADER

1) Grey, Zane, The Desert of Wheat, Harper & Brothers Publishers, New York, 1919.

Part Six — THE IDAHO NATIONAL HARVESTER

1) Moscow Evening Journal, Moscow, Idaho, August 9, 1906.

2) The Idaho Post, Moscow, Idaho, March 3, 1911.

3) The Star Mirror, Moscow, Idaho, April 29, 1909.

4) The Star Mirror, Moscow, Idaho, January 29, 1912.

5) Daily Star Mirror, Moscow, Idaho, September 4, 1912.

6) Daily Star Mirror, Moscow, Idaho, April 6, 1916.

7) University of Idaho Argonaut, Moscow, Idaho, August 3, 1923.

8) University of Idaho Argonaut, Moscow, Idaho, October 2, 1923.

9) Keith, T.B., When Mules and Horses Pushed. The Western Horseman, July, 1974, p. 60.

Other references:

The Idaho Post, Moscow, Idaho; January 19, 1912; July 7, 1916; July 19, 1918.

The Star Mirror, Moscow, Idaho; March 10, 1908; June 25, 1908; August 13, 1911.

Daily Star Mirror, Moscow, Idaho; January 19, 1912; February 10, 1912; September 14, 1912; October 28, 1912; March 6, 1916; March 12, 1916; March 16, 1916.

Part Seven — GREAT HORSEMEN

1) Clinton, Bruce, Riders North — Ropers South! Western Horseman, September-October, 1938.

2) Hammons, Mrs. Dorothy (Secretary), Pendleton Round-Up Association, Pendleton, Oregon, 1971.

3) Savitt, Sam, About Cowboys and Broncs, Arizona Highways V. LVI: 5, May, 1970.

4) Heston, Charlton, Yakima Canutt— Colfax Stunt Man is Called the Greatest. The Spokesman-Review, December 6, 1964.

5) Canutt, (Enos) Yakima, Personal Letter, 1970.

6) Shreve, George, Rodeo Fans Still Talk Reverently about the Fabled Jackson Sundown, Lewiston Morning Tribune, September 5, 1972.

7) Jackman, E.R. and R.A. Long, The Oregon Desert, Caxton Printers, Caldwell, Idaho, 1967.

8) Rancher is Expert at Desk Duty, Idahonian, Moscow, Idaho, June 12, 1964.

9) Stranger that Fiction is Appaloosa's Stamina, Idahonian, Moscow, Idaho, June 12, 1964.

10) Appaloosa is Unique Horse Name, Idahonian, Moscow, Idaho, June 12, 1964.

11) Horse on the Run, Western Livestock Journal, April, 1970.

12) Hubbard, Faye, Personal Letter, August, 1973.

13) Epic Drama of the West. The Pendleton Round-Up, 1929.

14) Furlong, Charles Wellington, Let'er Buck, A Story of the Passing of the Old West. C. P. Putnam's Sons, New York and London. The Knickerbocker Press, 1921.

15) Laughlin, J.J., Personal Letter.

Part Eight — POST HORSE ERA

1) Manufacturers of farm traction steam engines are listed by Reynold M. Wik, *Steam Power on the American Farm* (University of Pennsylvania Press, 1953), pp. 254-5.

2) Beresford, Hobart, "Power Alcohol from Farm Products"; in *Papers of the Pacific Northwest Chemurgic Conference* (1937), p. 190.

3) "Can yesterday's farming feed today's people?", *Crops and Soils Magazine,* December 1975, pp. 5-8.

4) Wooley, J.C., "Pioneer agriculture to fantastic farming in my time" (typescript, c. 1970), p. 33.

5) Hatley, George B. Pack Horses, Secretary of the Appaloosa Horse Club, Moscow, Idaho.

6) Hatley, George B. Appaloosa Horse Club, Secretary of the Appaloosa Horse Club, Moscow Idaho.